FACES OF HARLEY

Richard B. Ressman, M.D.

OTHER BOOKS BY RICHARD B. RESSMAN

Lines & Curves

Lines & Curves 2

Godiva: A Modern Pictorial Adventure

The Wall of Fame

FACES OF HARLEY

Richard B. Ressman, M.D.

Coyote Creek Books | San José | California

Copyright © 2017 by Richard B. Ressman. All rights reserved.

No part of this book may be reproduced or transmitted in any form by any means, electronic or mechanical, including photocopying, recording, or by any information storage and retrieval system, without written permission from the publisher, except for the inclusion of brief quotations in a review.

All photos © Richard B. Ressman.

Printed in the United States of America.

ISBN-978-1946647108

Published by Coyote Creek Books
www.coyotecreek.books.com

This book is dedicated to Gabriele.

ABOUT THE AUTHOR

Dr. Richard Ressman practiced orthopaedic surgery for thirty years before becoming a full time professional photographer. The replacing of hips and knees as well as performing arthroscopic surgical procedures of the knee is now replaced by the use of cameras and strobes, tripods and monopods to complete the capture of his current subjects.

PREFACE

On the one hundredth anniversary of the Harley-Davidson Motorcycle Company in Milwaukee, Wisconsin, I had the opportunity to be one of the invited photographers. I met and photographed motorcycle enthusiasts and attendees from all over the world attending this special event. Harleys are a significant part of Americana. Photos paired with quotes and facts are presented showing an aspect of the Harley Culture that many don't get to see.

Harley-Davidson Founders

William S. Harley
Arthur Davidson
Walter Davidson
William A. Davidson

Headquarters
Milwaukee, Wisconsin

1903

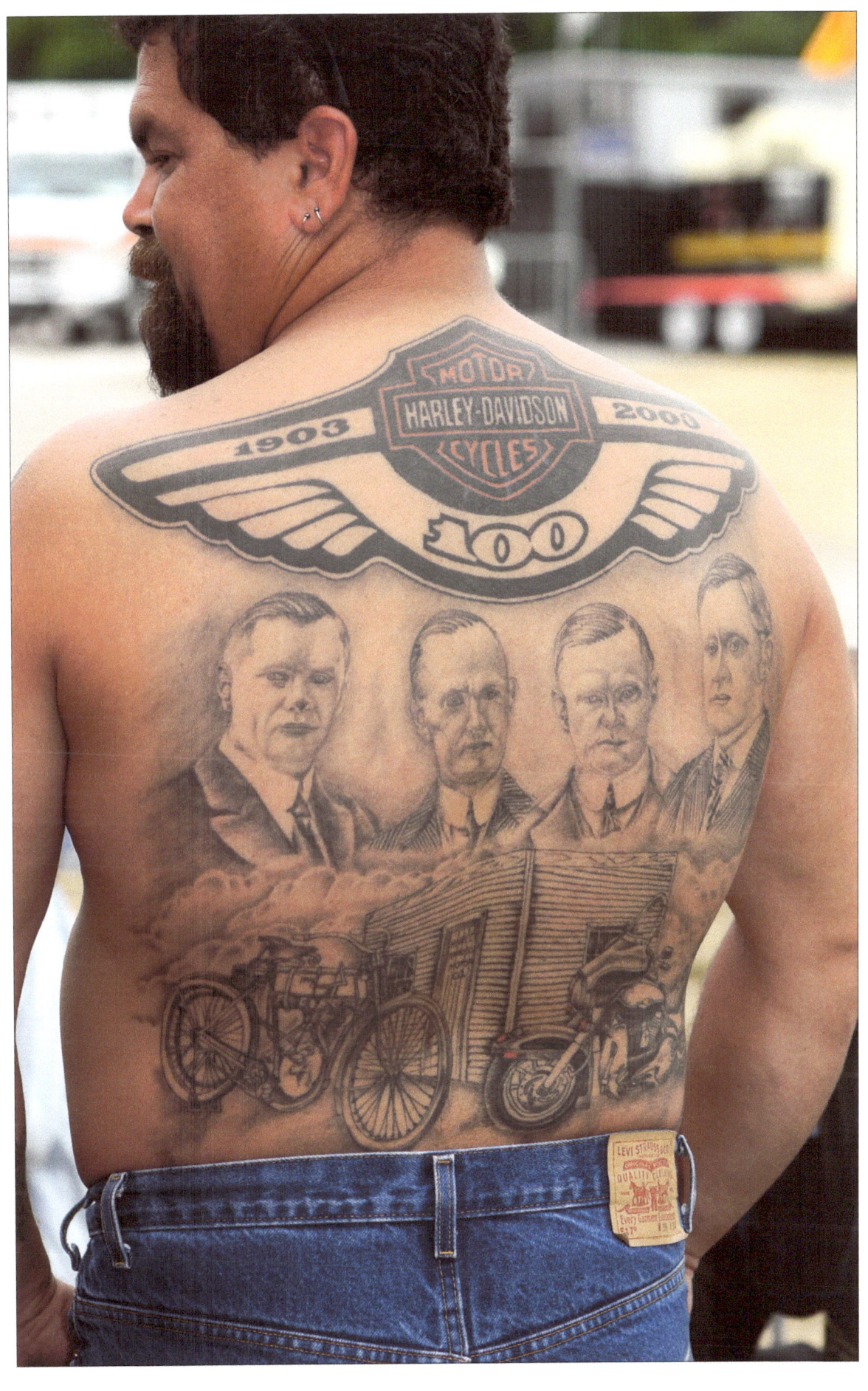

FACES OF HARLEY

Only a Harley sounds like a Harley

    It's as distinctive as a human voice.

        As memorable as a kiss

Put any muffler you want on it-

    or none at all.

        And it will still sound

uniquely like a Harley-Davidson.

        —Harley-Davidson Website

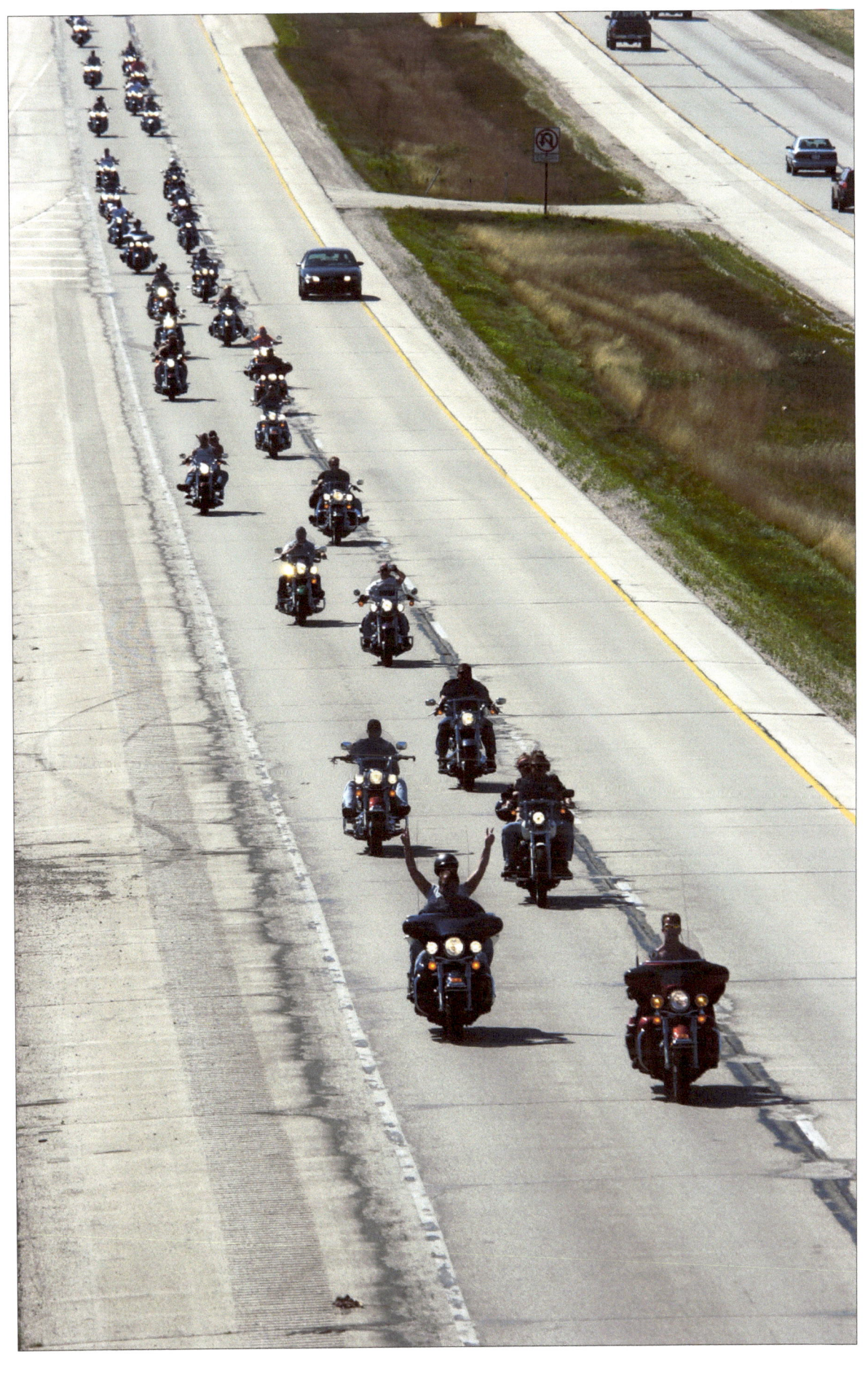

FACES OF HARLEY

Riding a Harley-Davidson may be the last pure expression

of what it means to be an American.

The freedom to go somewhere. Anywhere.

Just you and the road and the wind and an engine

that growls POTATO, POTATO, POTATO.

—Harley-Davidson Website

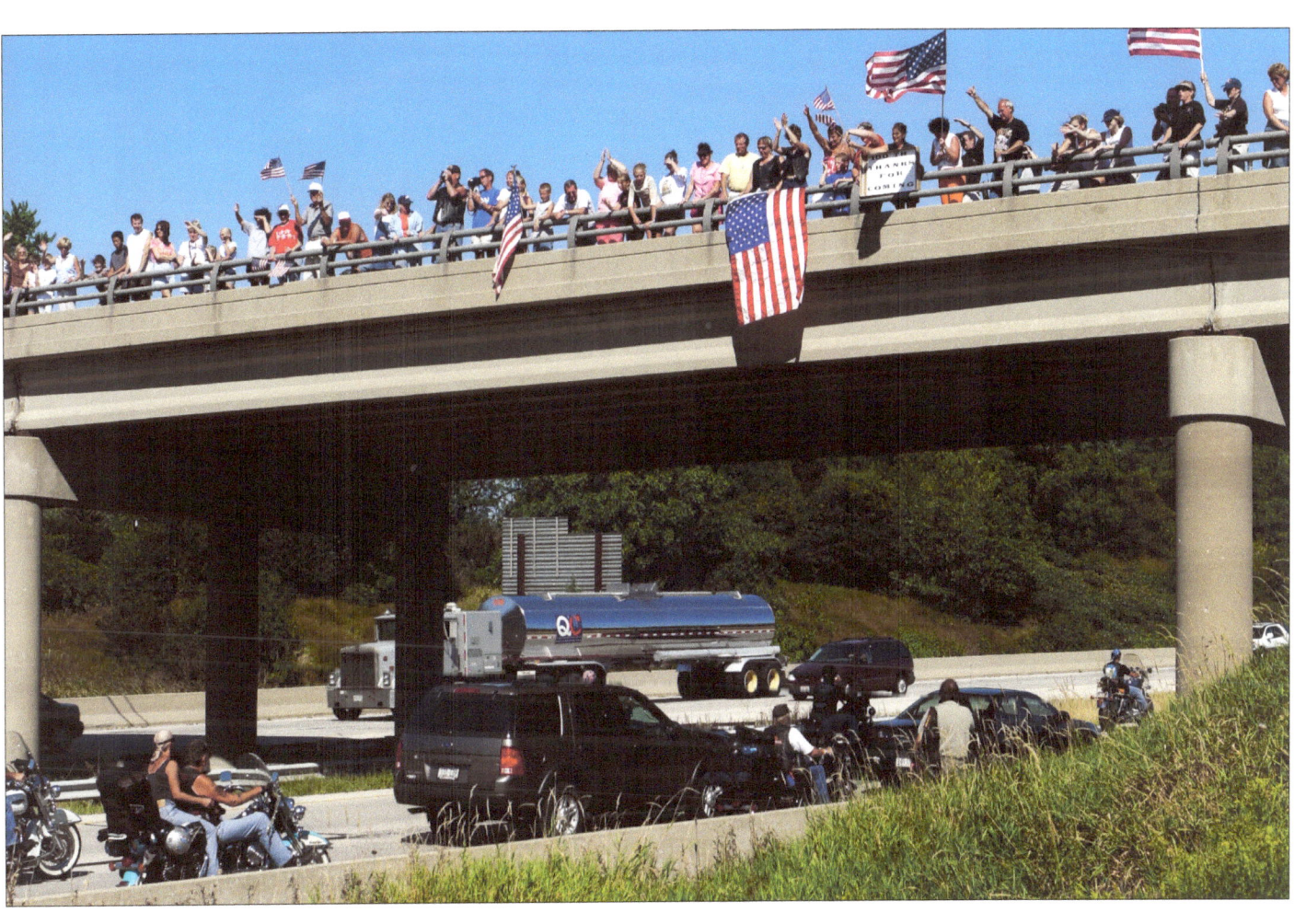

FACES OF HARLEY

Harley Mystique is

    a reflection of Americana…

The most overwhelming feeling

    from riding a Harley is

        a sense of belonging.

           —Steve Lysonski

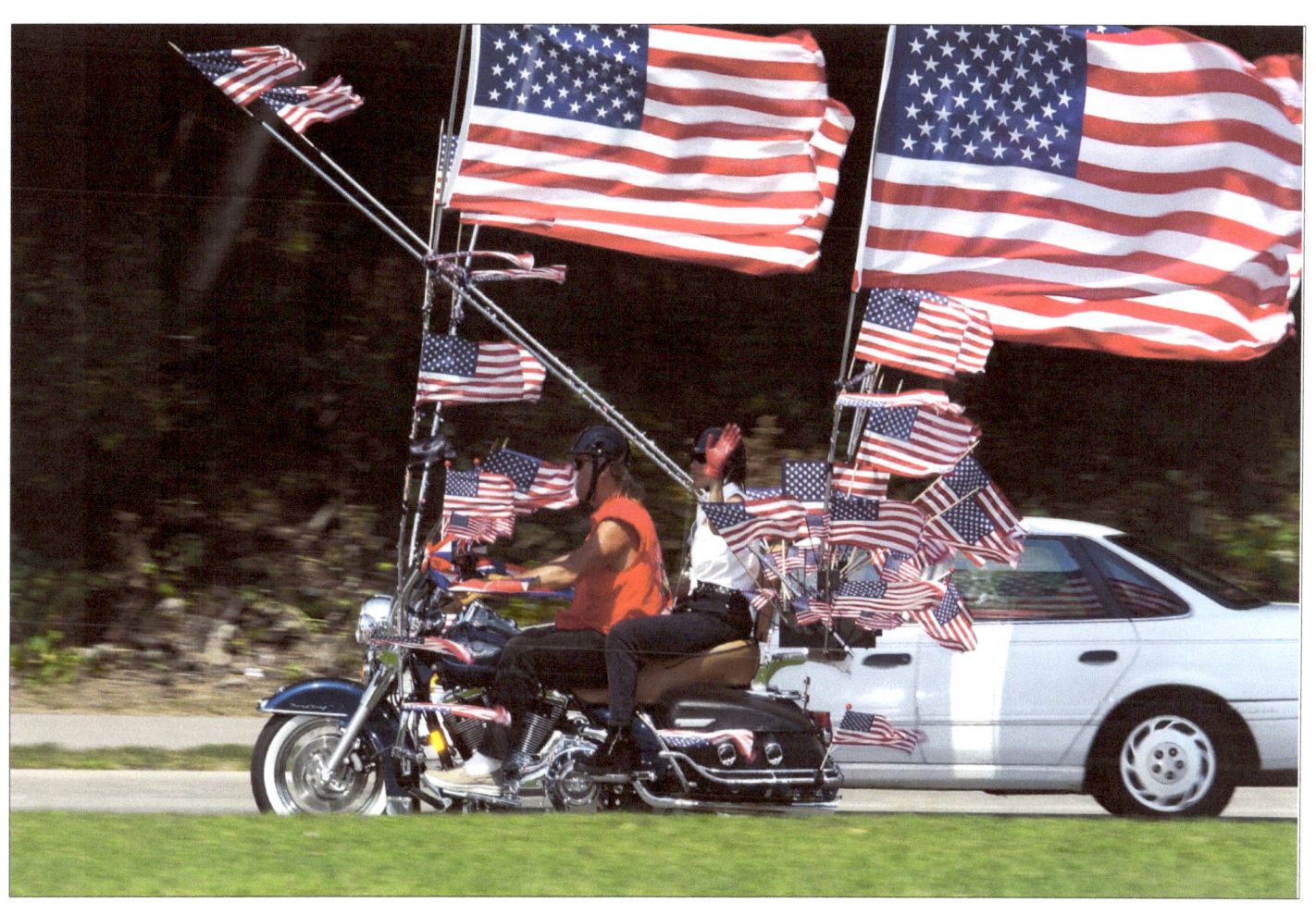

Keep your bike in good repair:

    motorcycle boots are not comfortable for walking.

        —Author Unknown

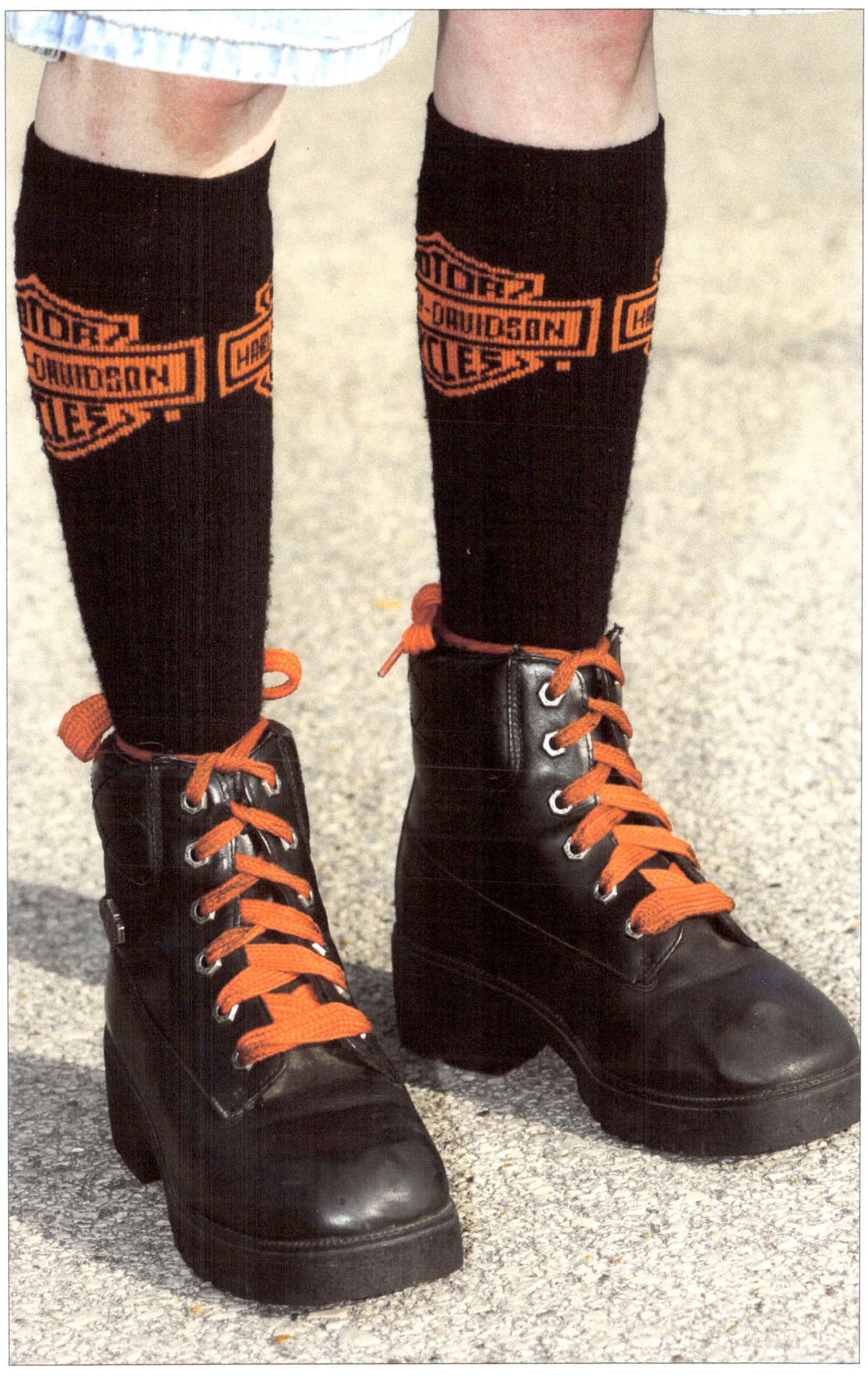

FACES OF HARLEY

The average Harley rider is

    whoever owns one, whoever rides one.

The rest doesn't matter—

    Mostly it just feels good and is a stress reliever.

        —Cindy Swift

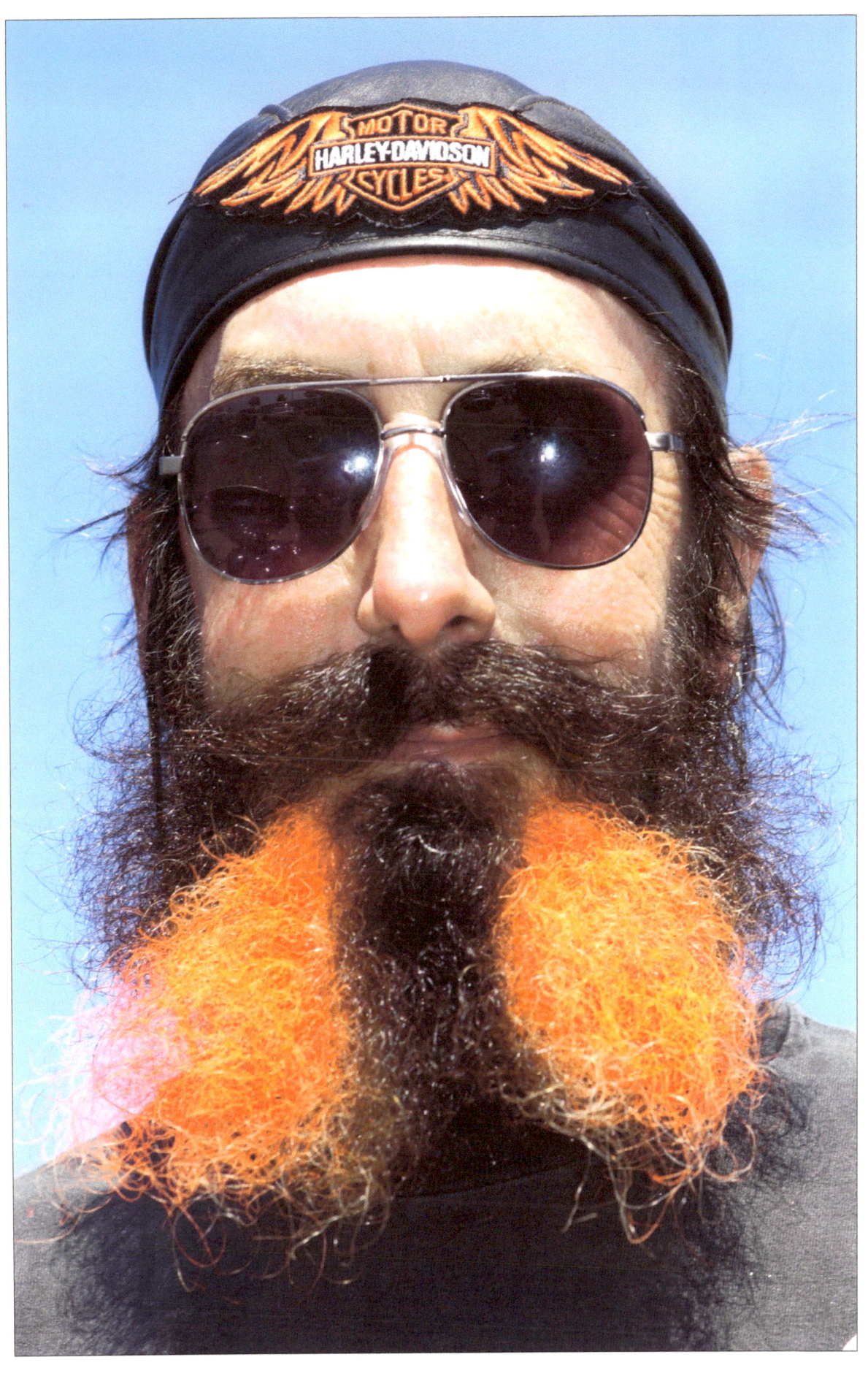

Four wheels

      move the body.

Two wheels

      move the soul.

           —Author unknown

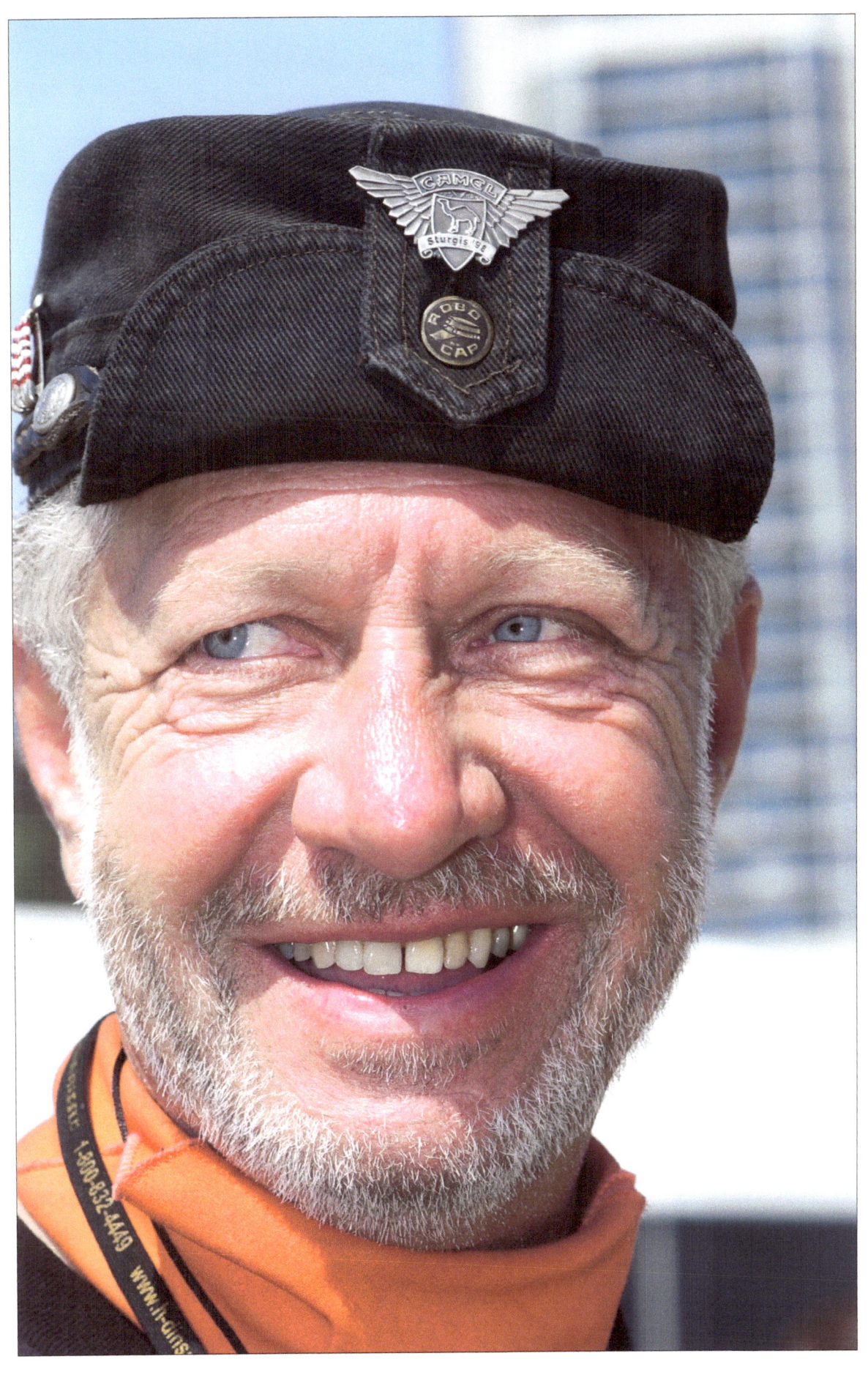

FACES OF HARLEY

A good long ride can clear your mind,

restore your faith,

and use up a lot of fuel.

—Author unknown

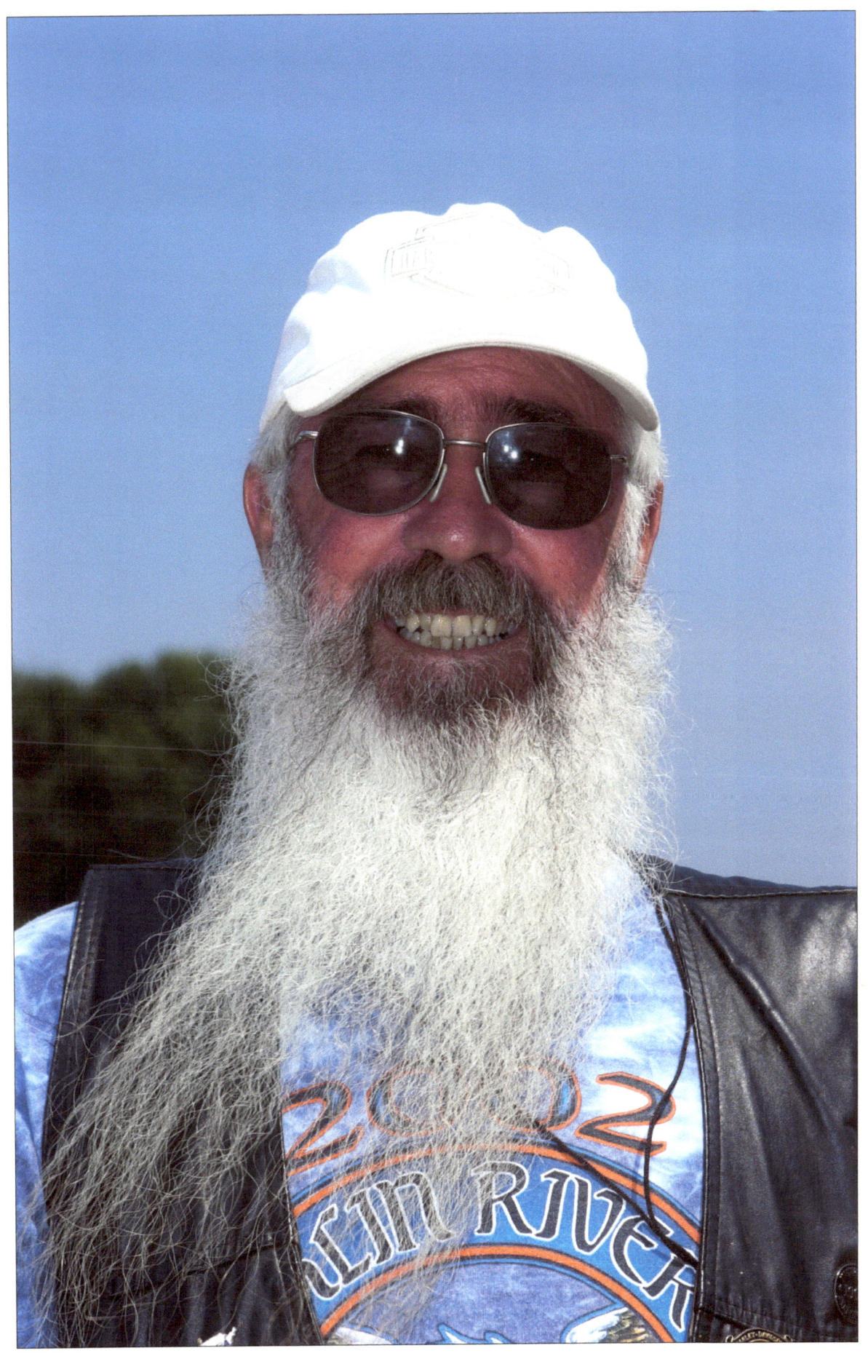

The perfect man?

A poet on a motorcycle.

—Lucinda Williams

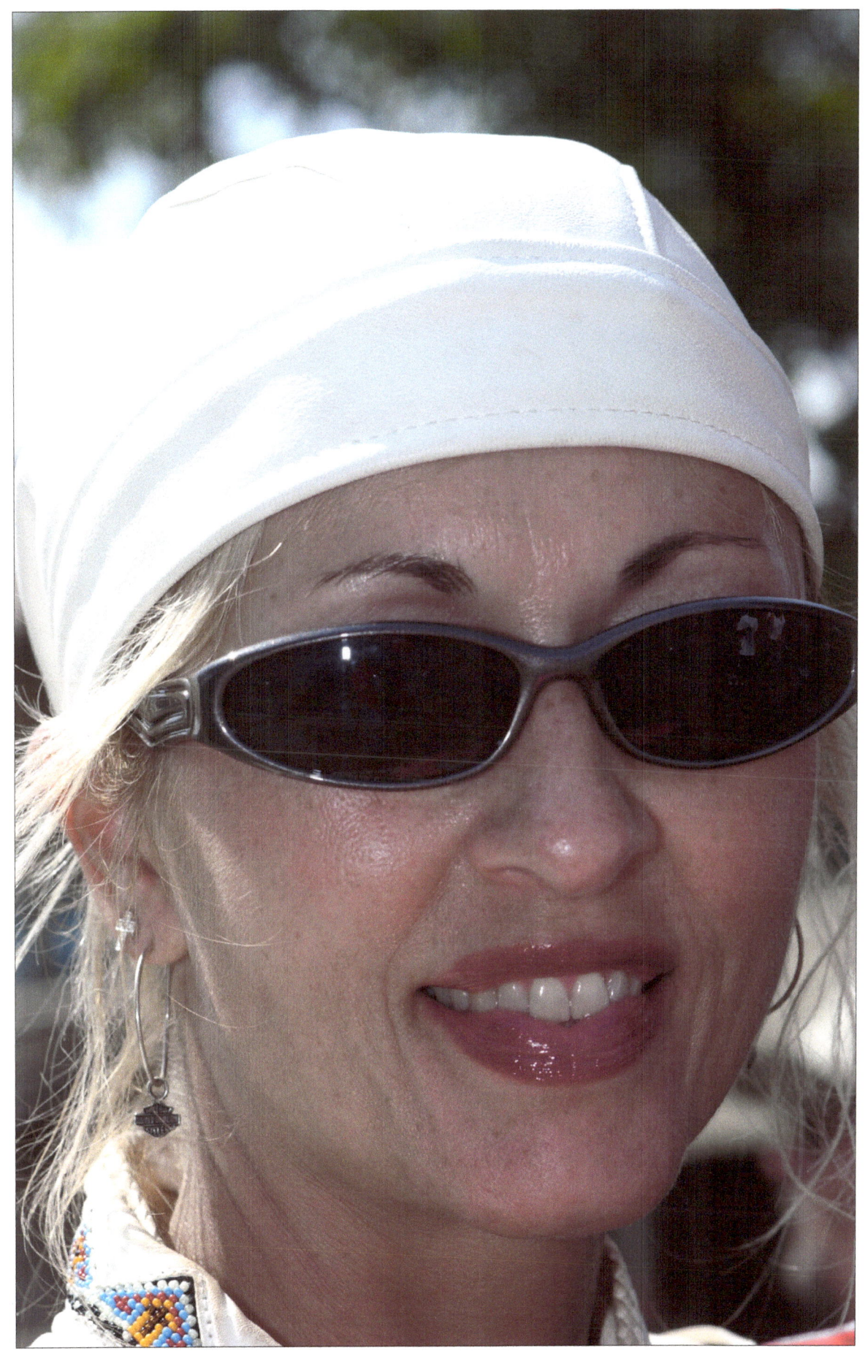

If you don't ride in the rain,

you don't ride.

—Author Unknown

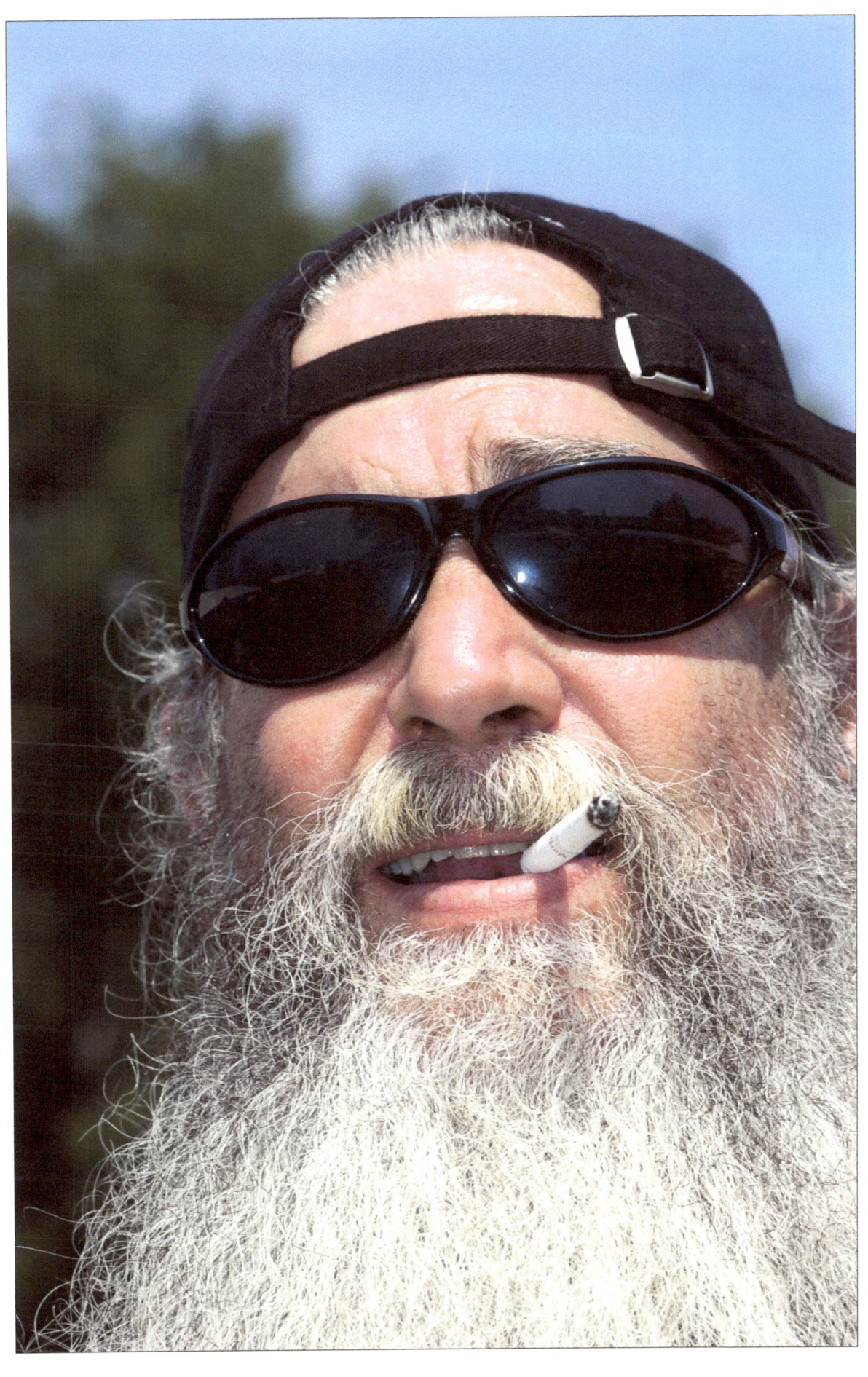

FACES OF HARLEY

Gray-haired riders

don't get that way

from pure luck.

—Author unknown

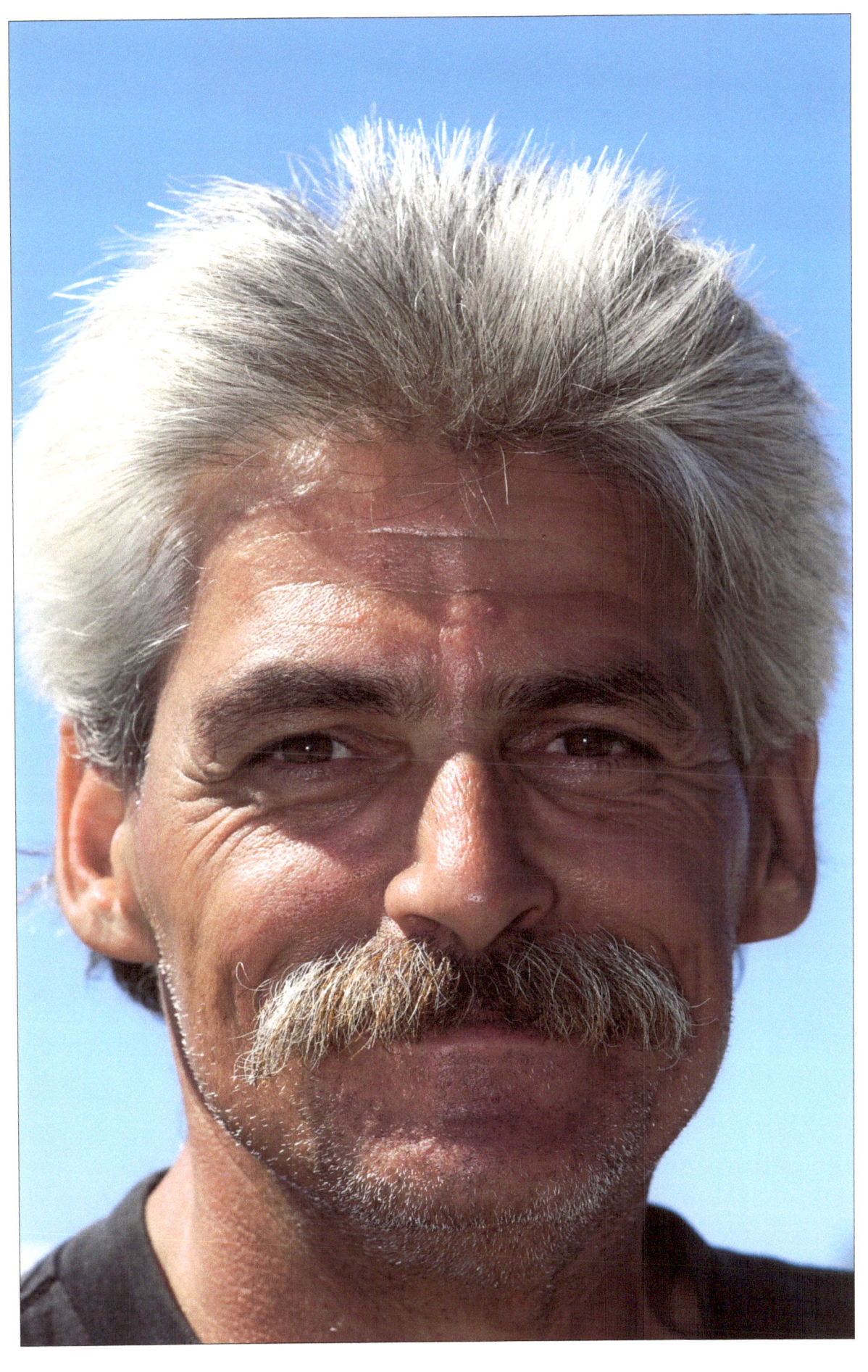

FACES OF HARLEY

That's all the motorcycle is,

a system of concepts worked out in steel.

—Robert M. Pirsig, *Zen and the Art of Motorcycle Maintenance*

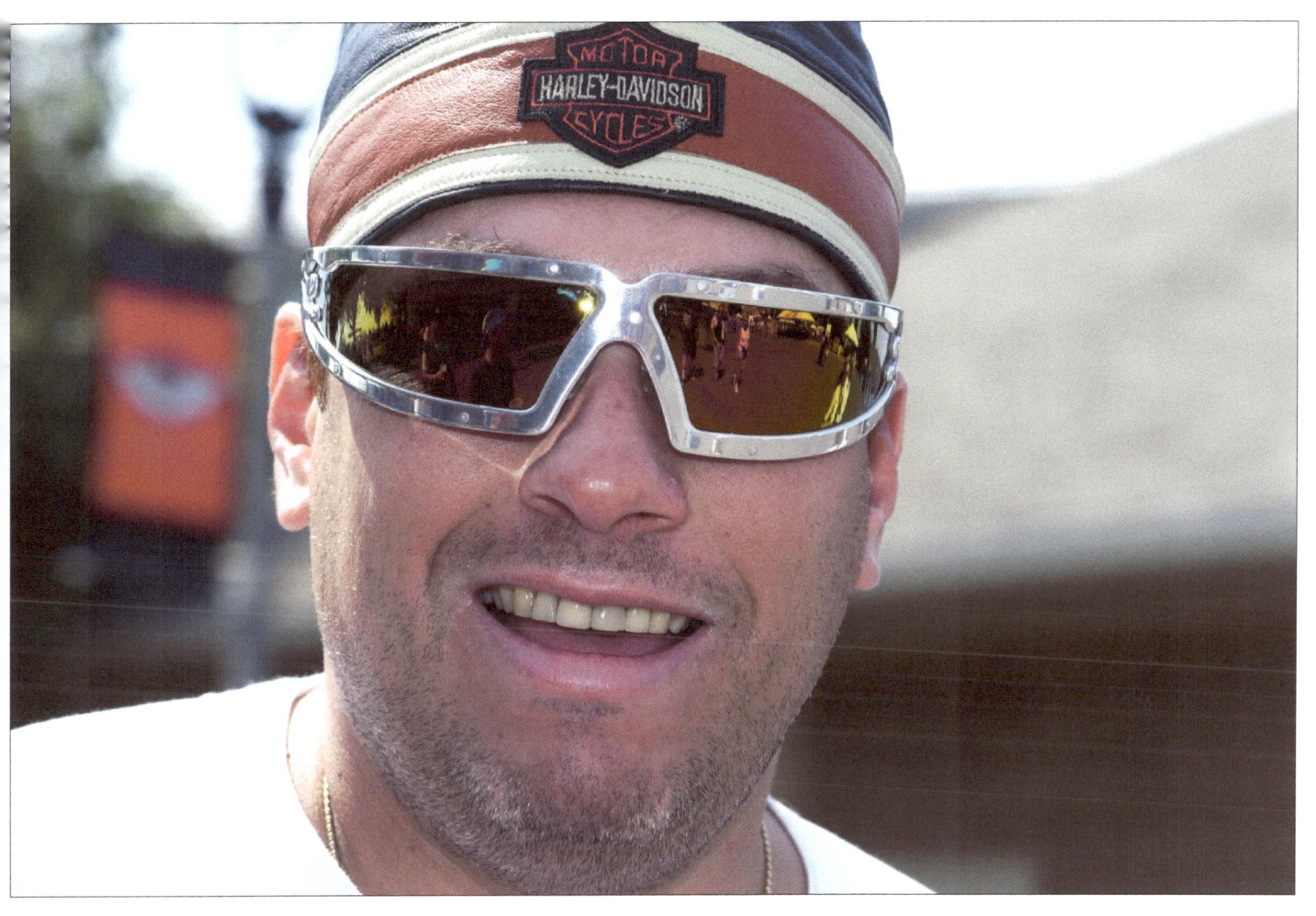

Forget a knight in shining armor…

I'll take a biker in dirty leathers

any day!

—Author unknown

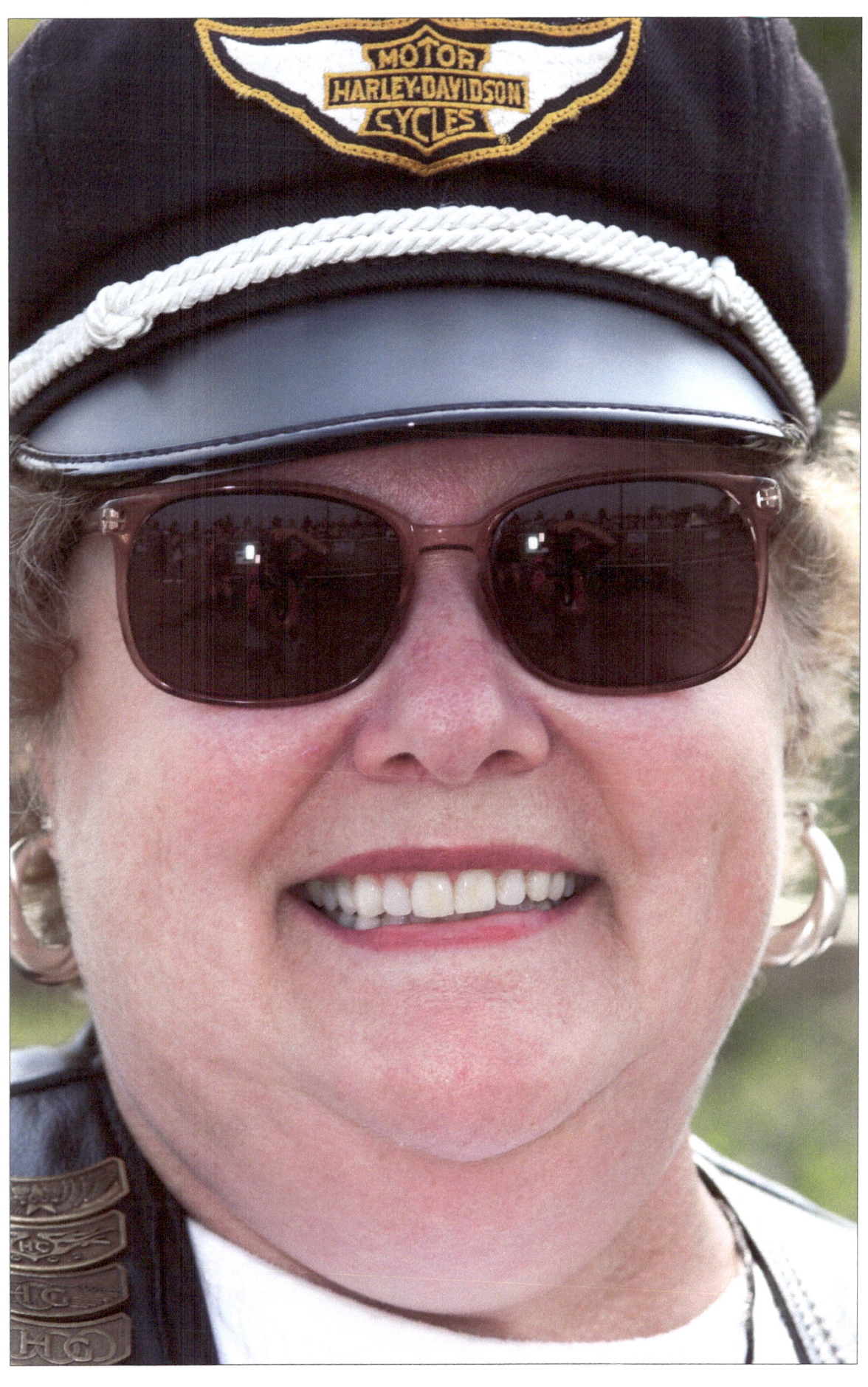

FACES OF HARLEY

When life throws you a curve…

lean into it.

—Author unknown

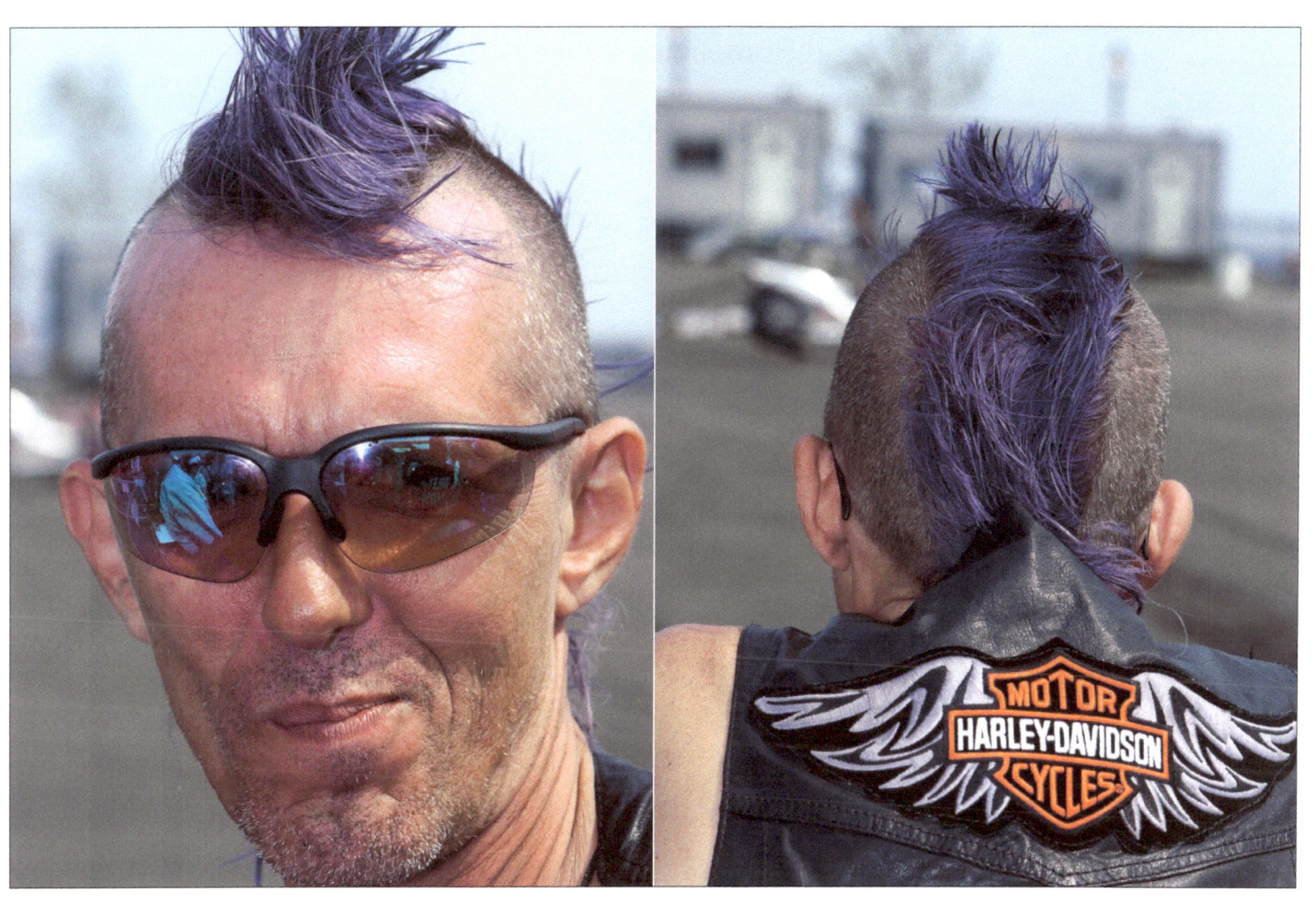

Sometimes it takes

a whole tankful of fuel

before you

can think straight.

—Author unknown

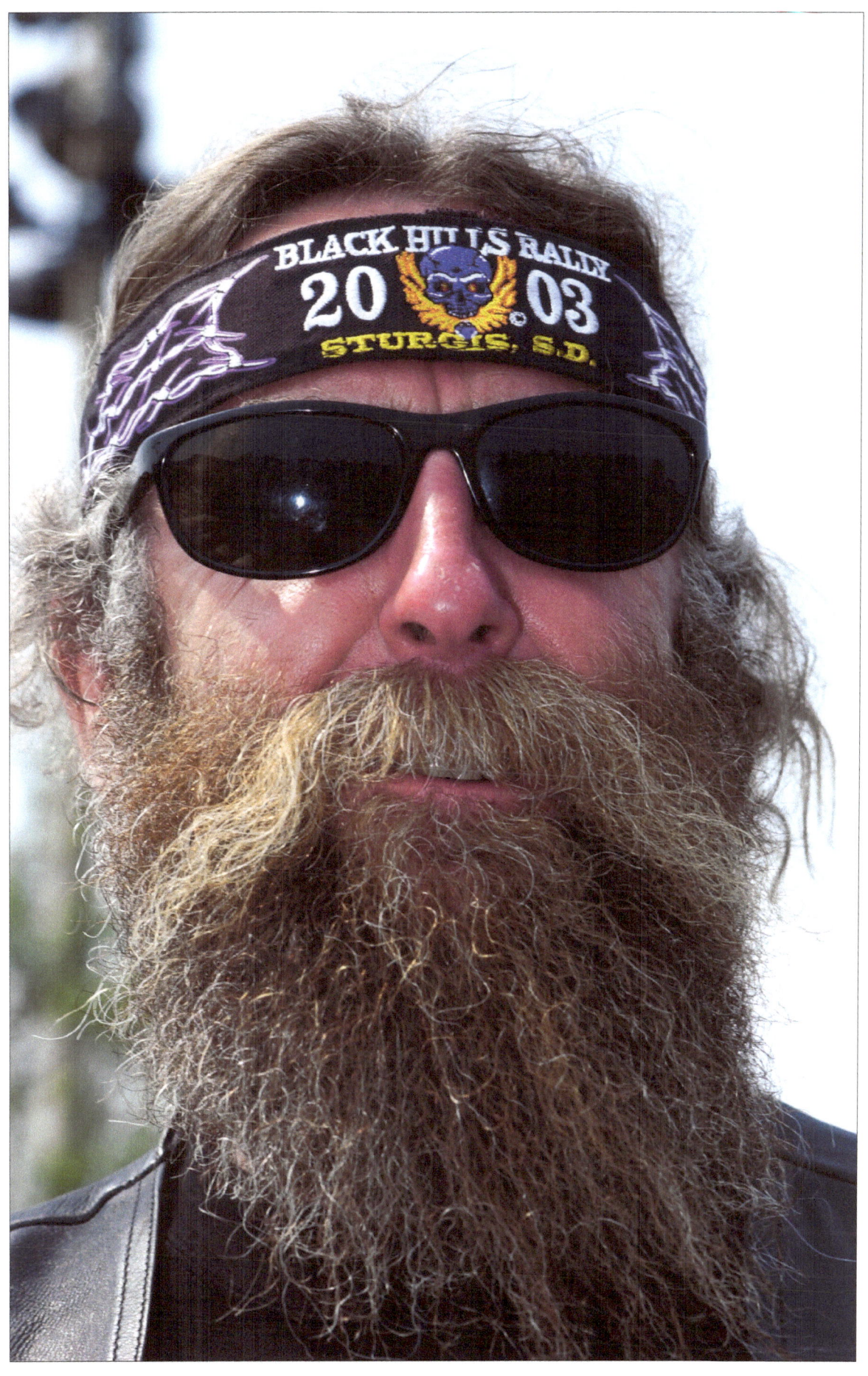

Whatever it is,

it's better

in the wind.

—Author Unknown

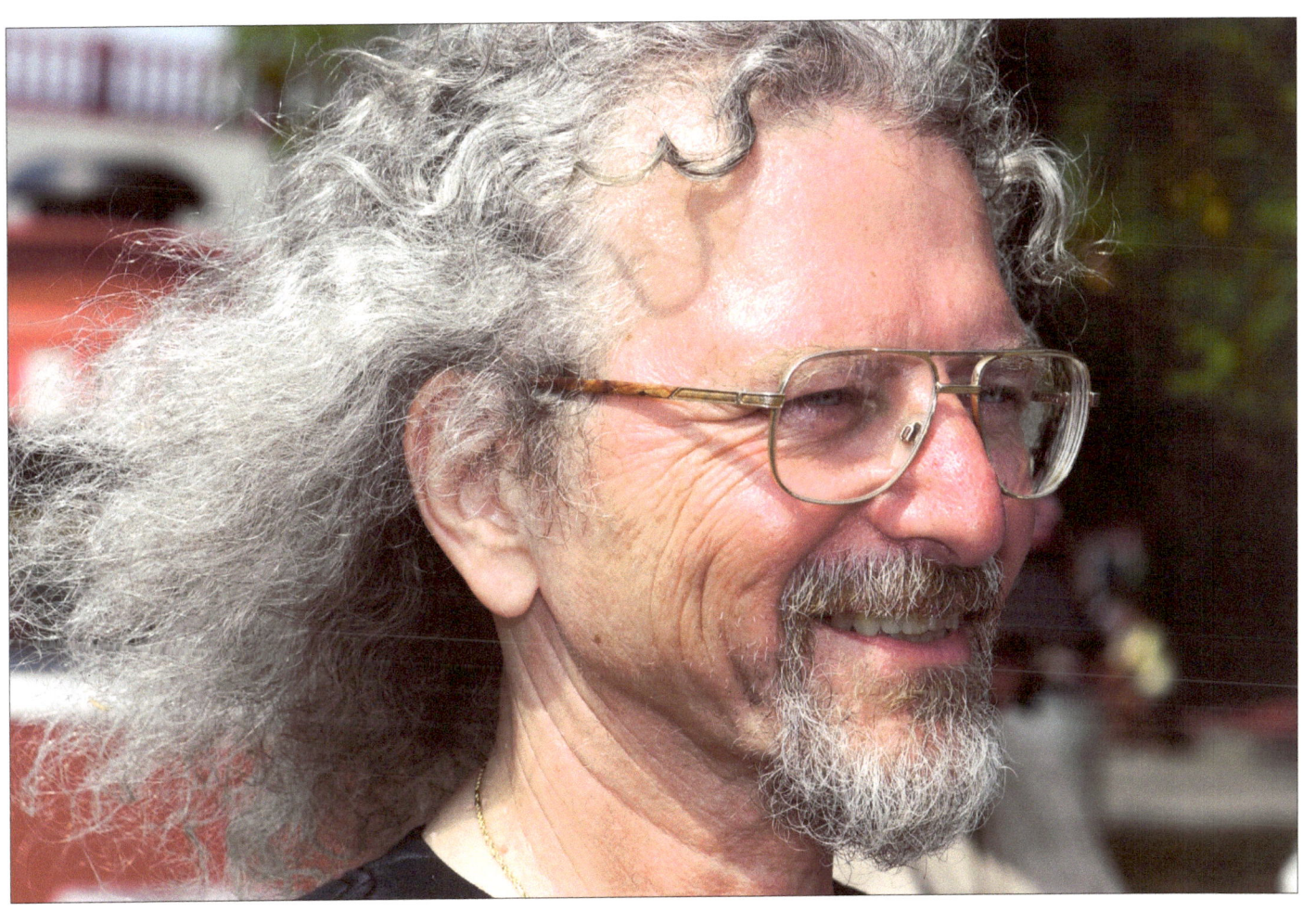

Safety is a cheap and effective

insurance policy

—Author unknown

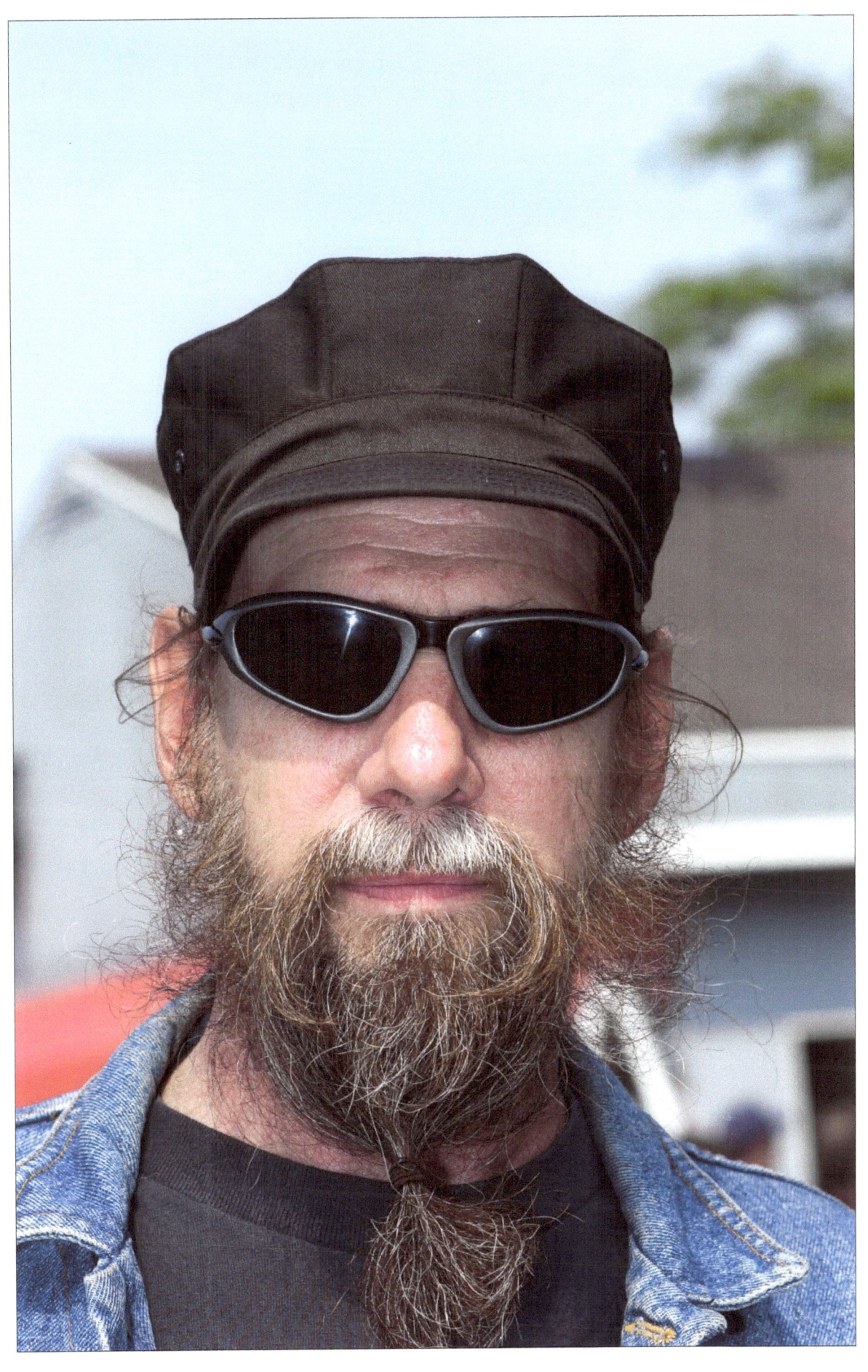

Respect the person

who has seen the dark side

of motorcycling

and lived.

—Author unknown

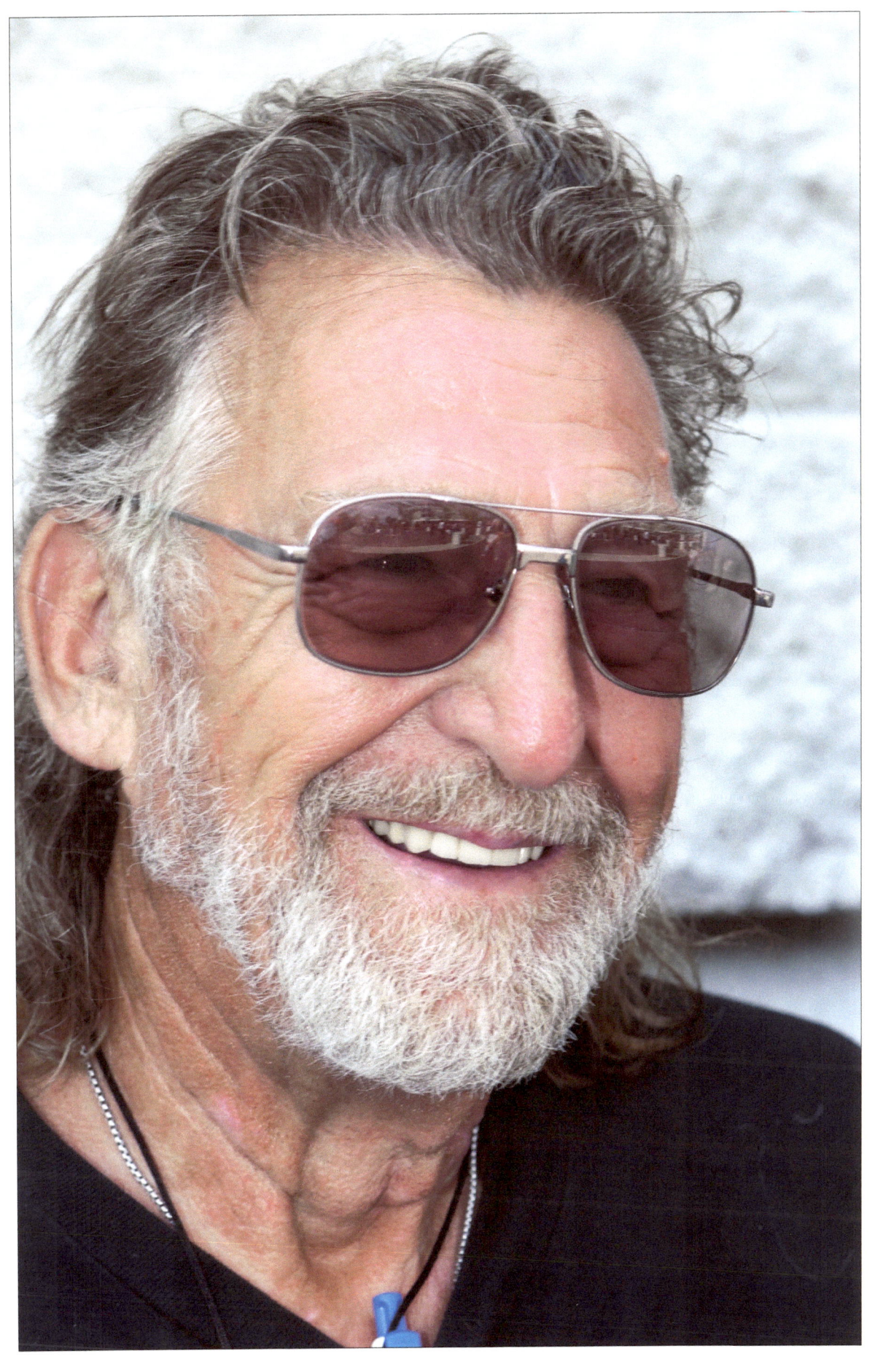

A friend is someone

    who'll get out of bed at 2 am

        to drive his pickup

to the middle of nowhere

    to get you when

        you're broken down.

            —Author unknown

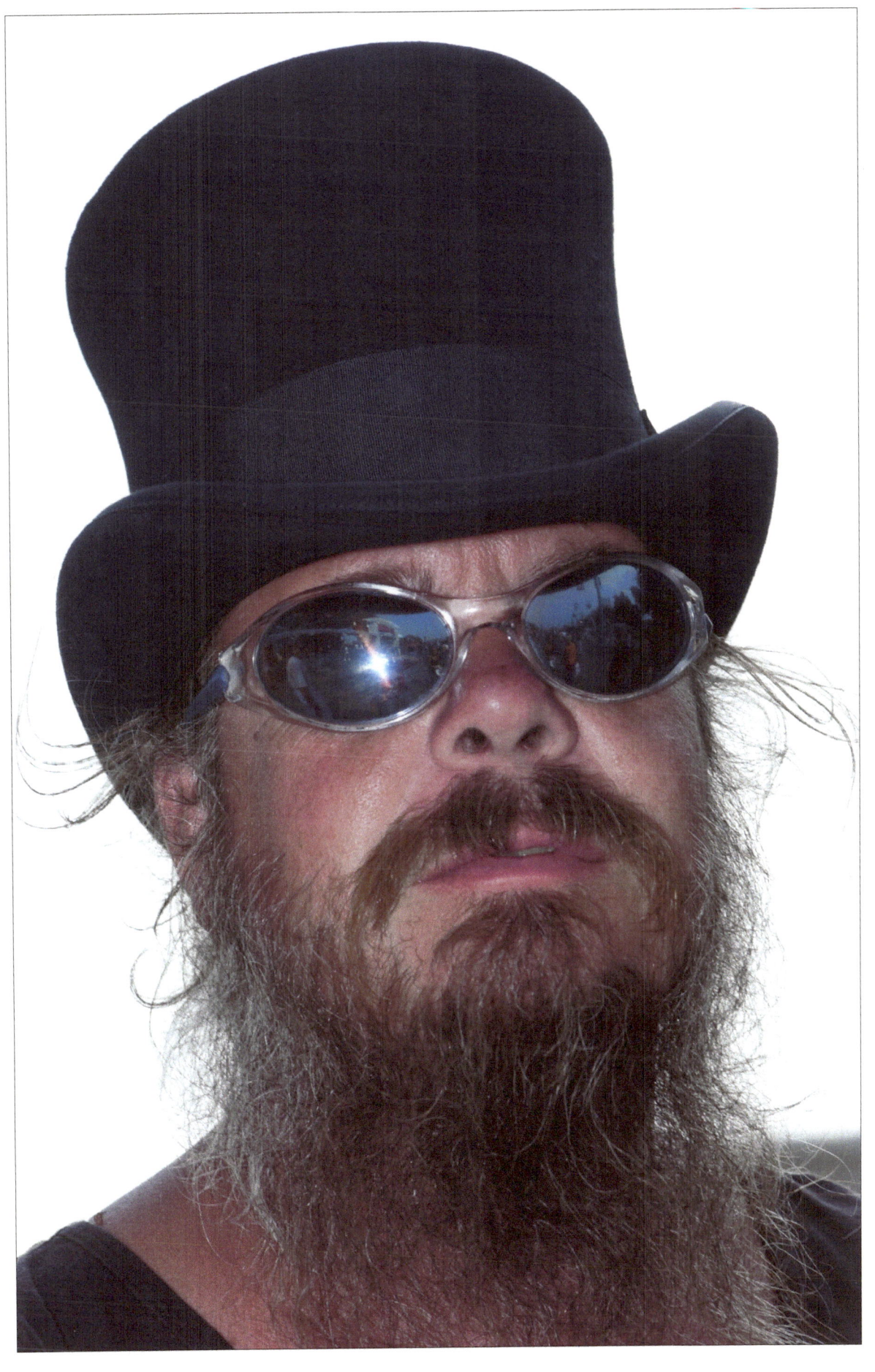

Faster, faster, faster,

until the thrill of speed

overcomes the fear of death.

—Hunter S. Thompson

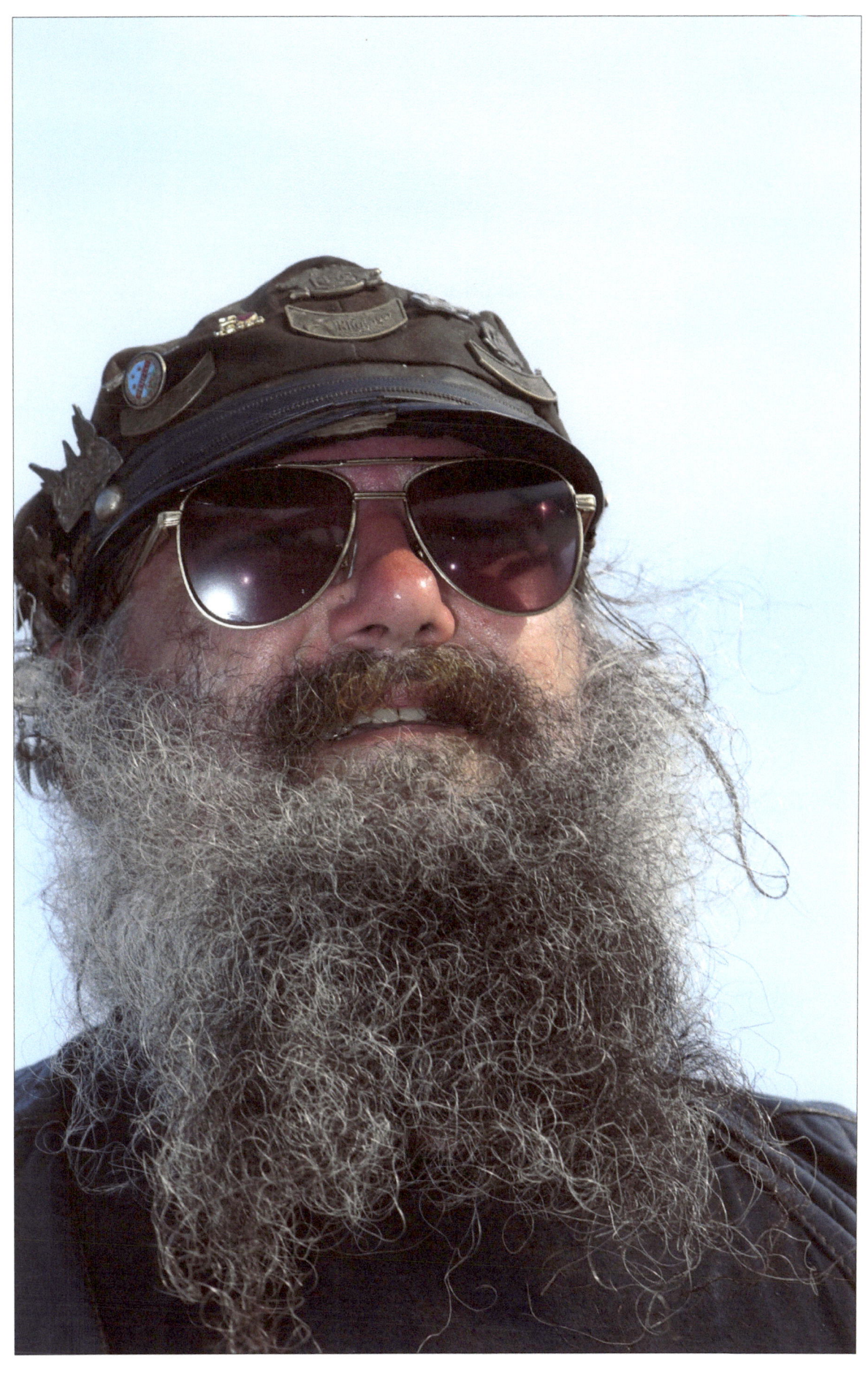

If she changes her oil

more than she

changes her mind,

follow her.

—Author unknown

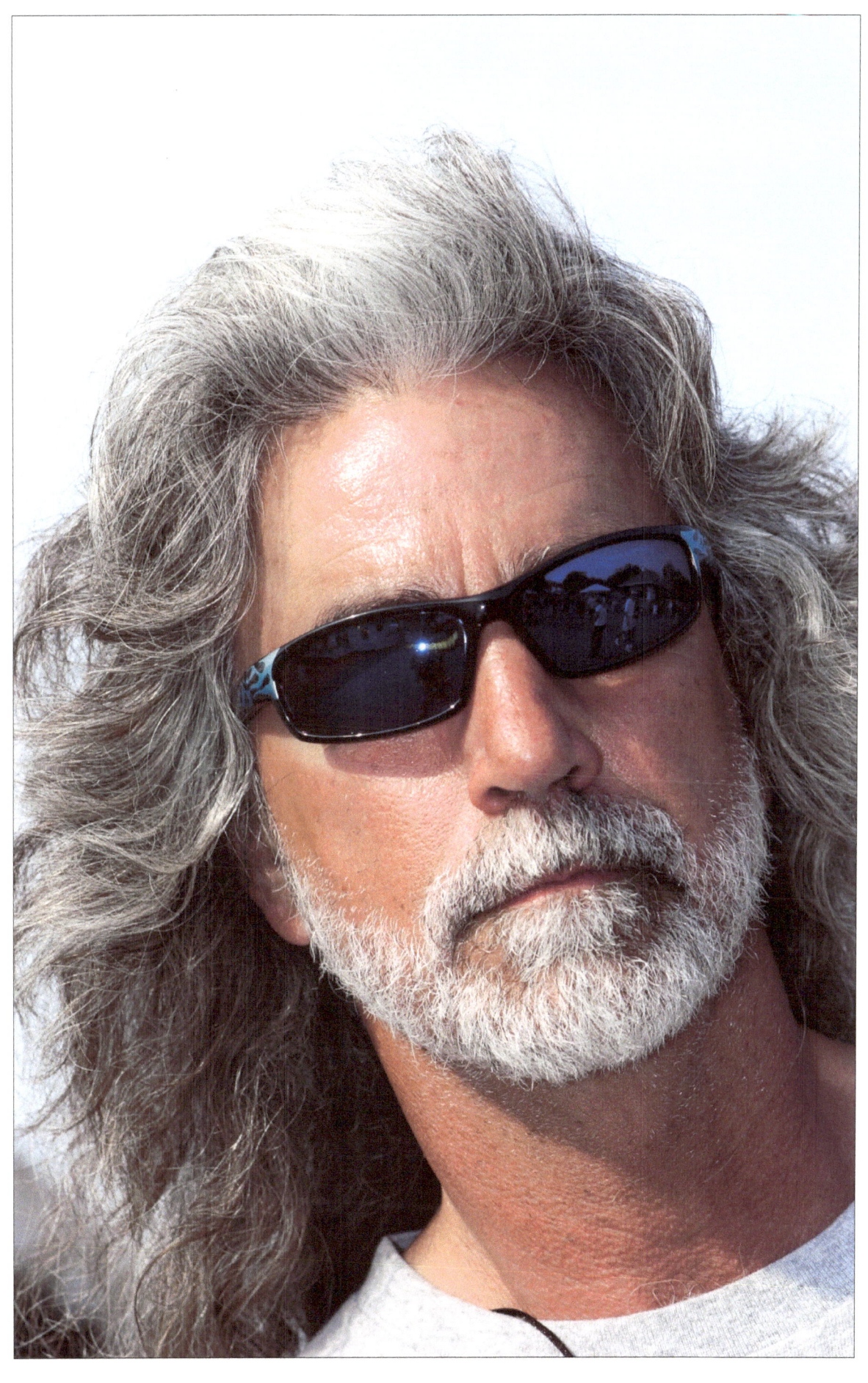

FACES OF HARLEY

I don't want a pickle...

Just want to ride on

my motorcycle.

—Arlo Guthrie

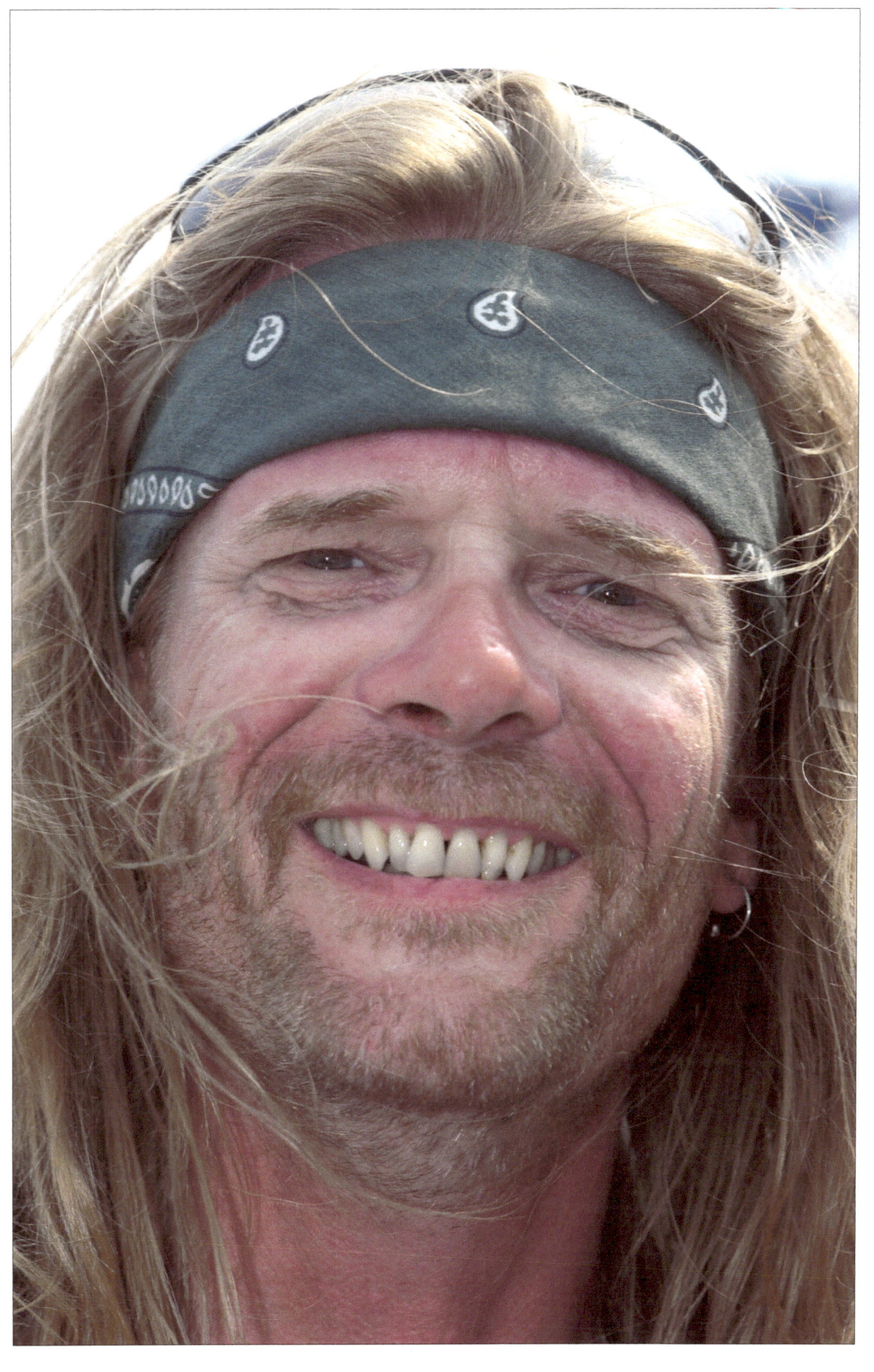

Midnight bugs taste best.

—Author unknown

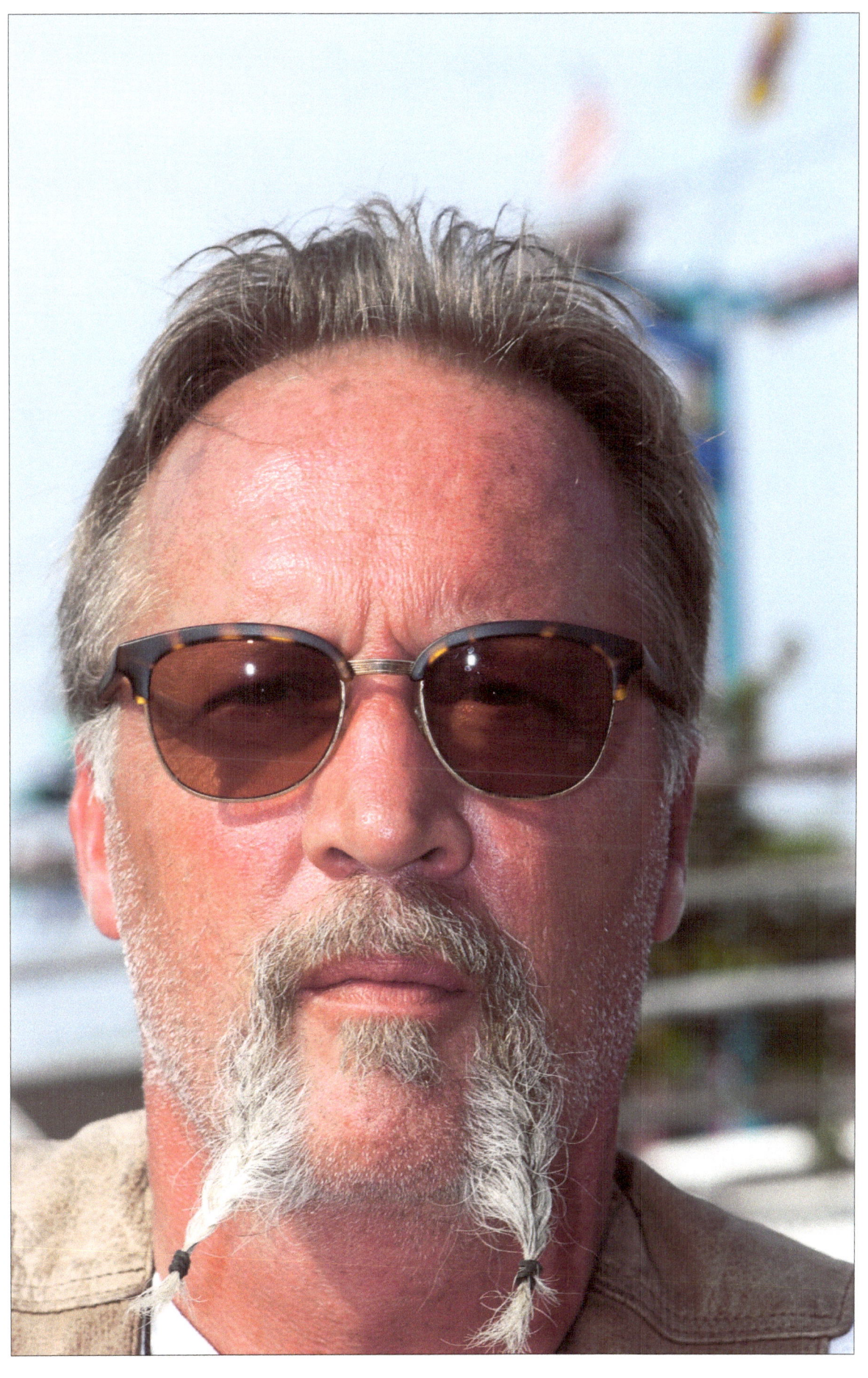

FACES OF HARLEY

Growing old is mandatory,

but growing up is optional.

—Anon

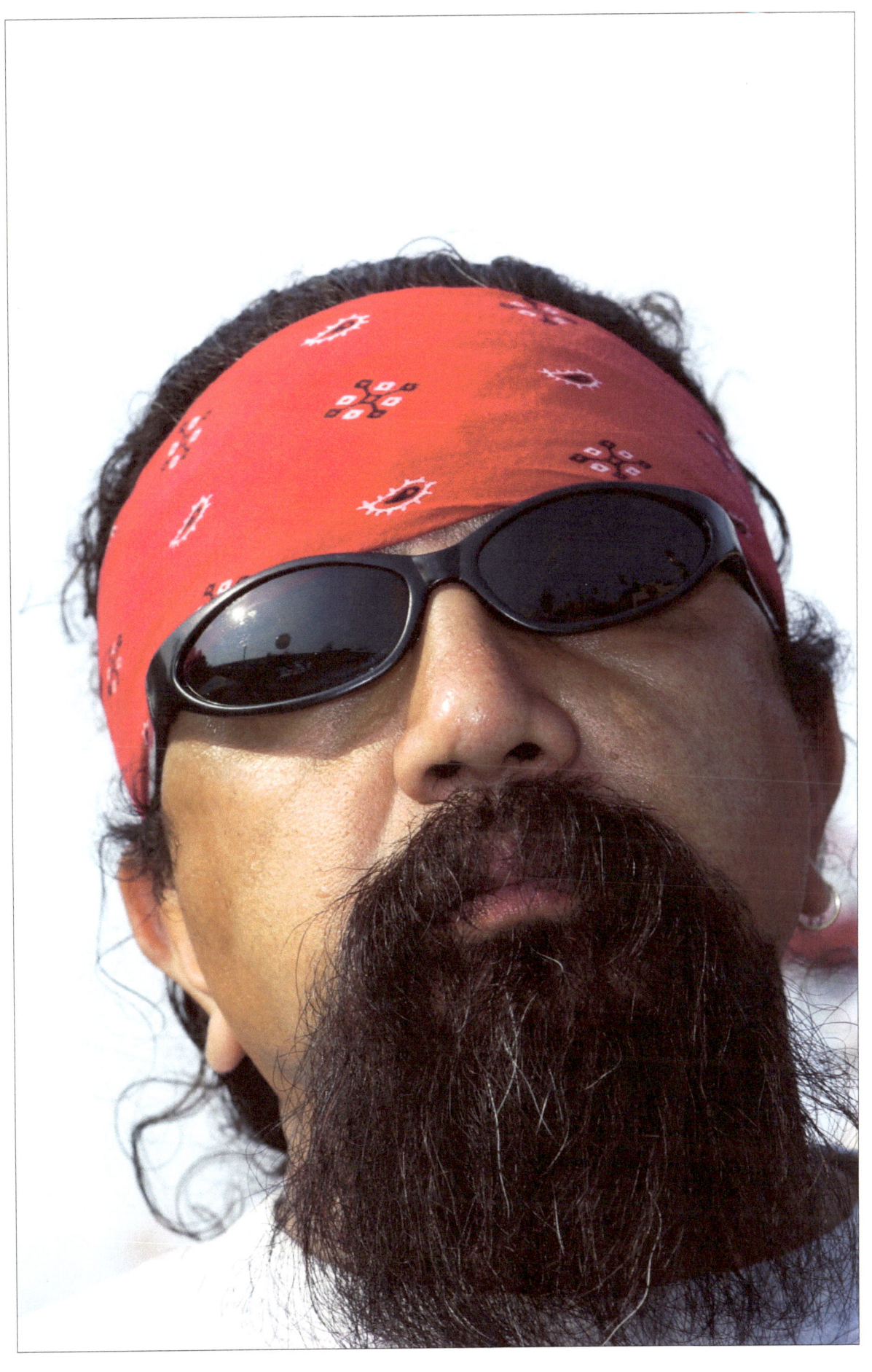

FACES OF HARLEY

Life may begin at 30,

    but it doesn't get

        real interesting

            until about 150.

                —Author Unknown

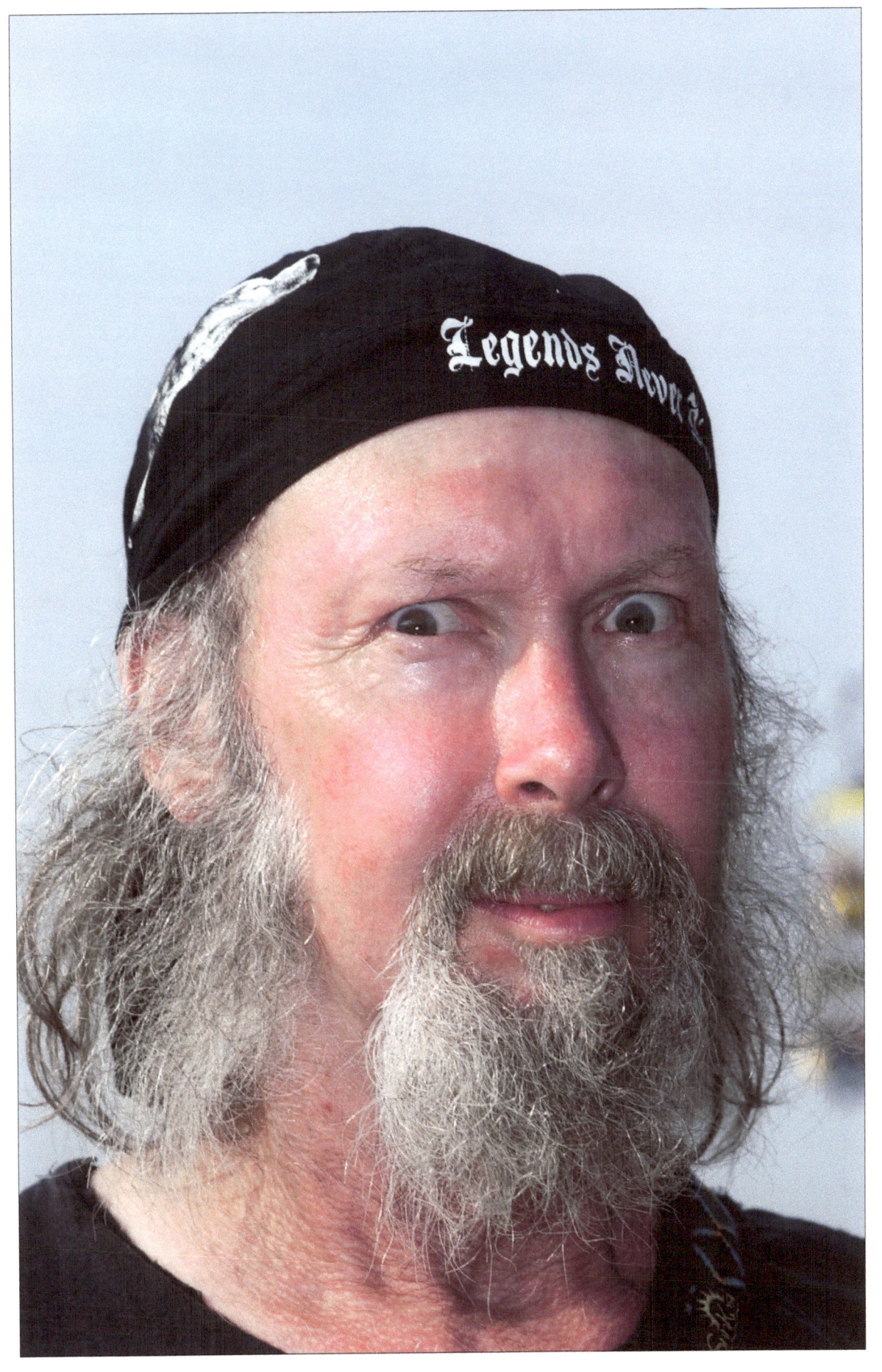

200 mph, no hands.

Damn that'd be cool...

right up to the part

where you die.

—A. Duthie

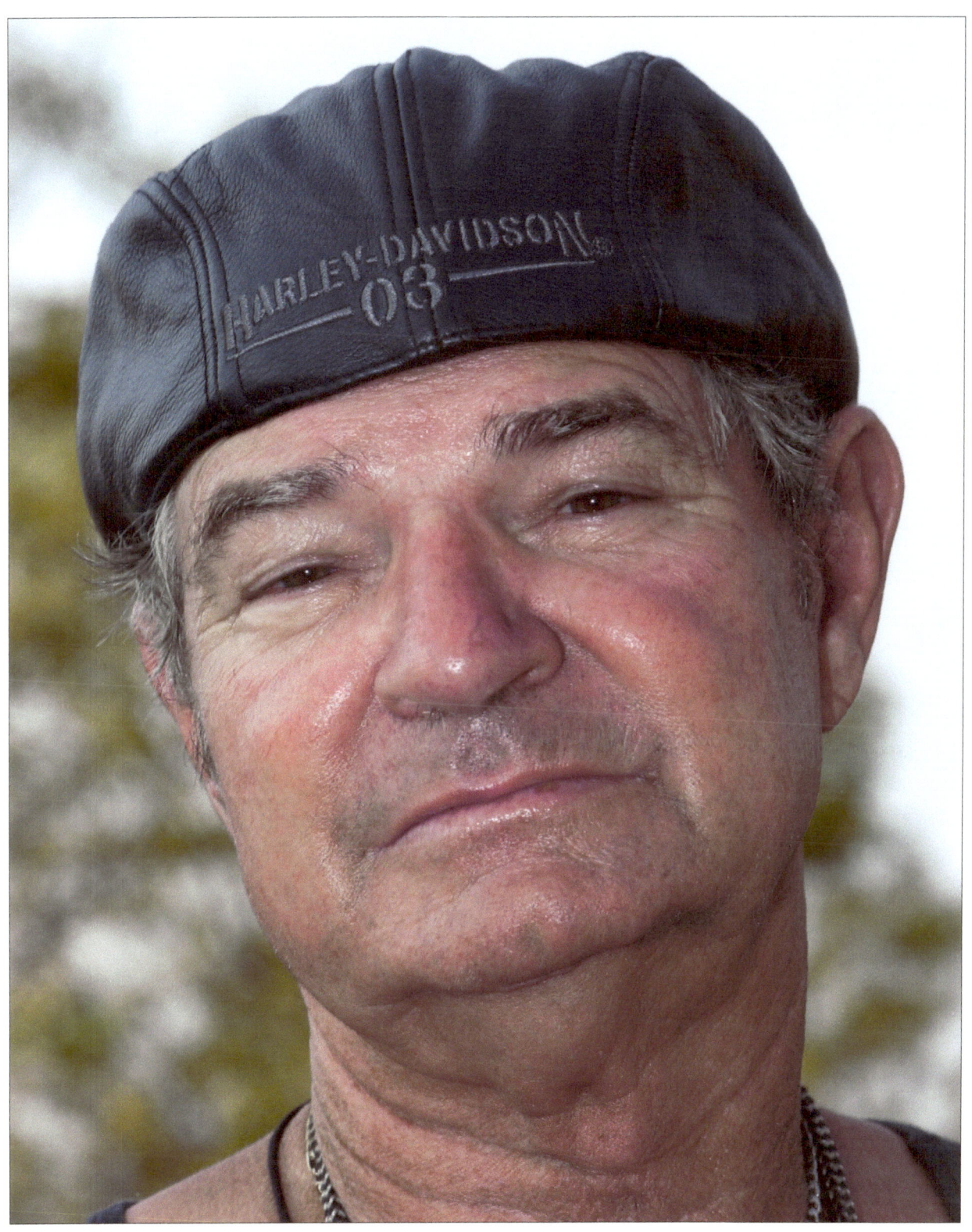

Hop on your steel horse and

go find your soul in the wind.

—Steel Cowgirls LLC

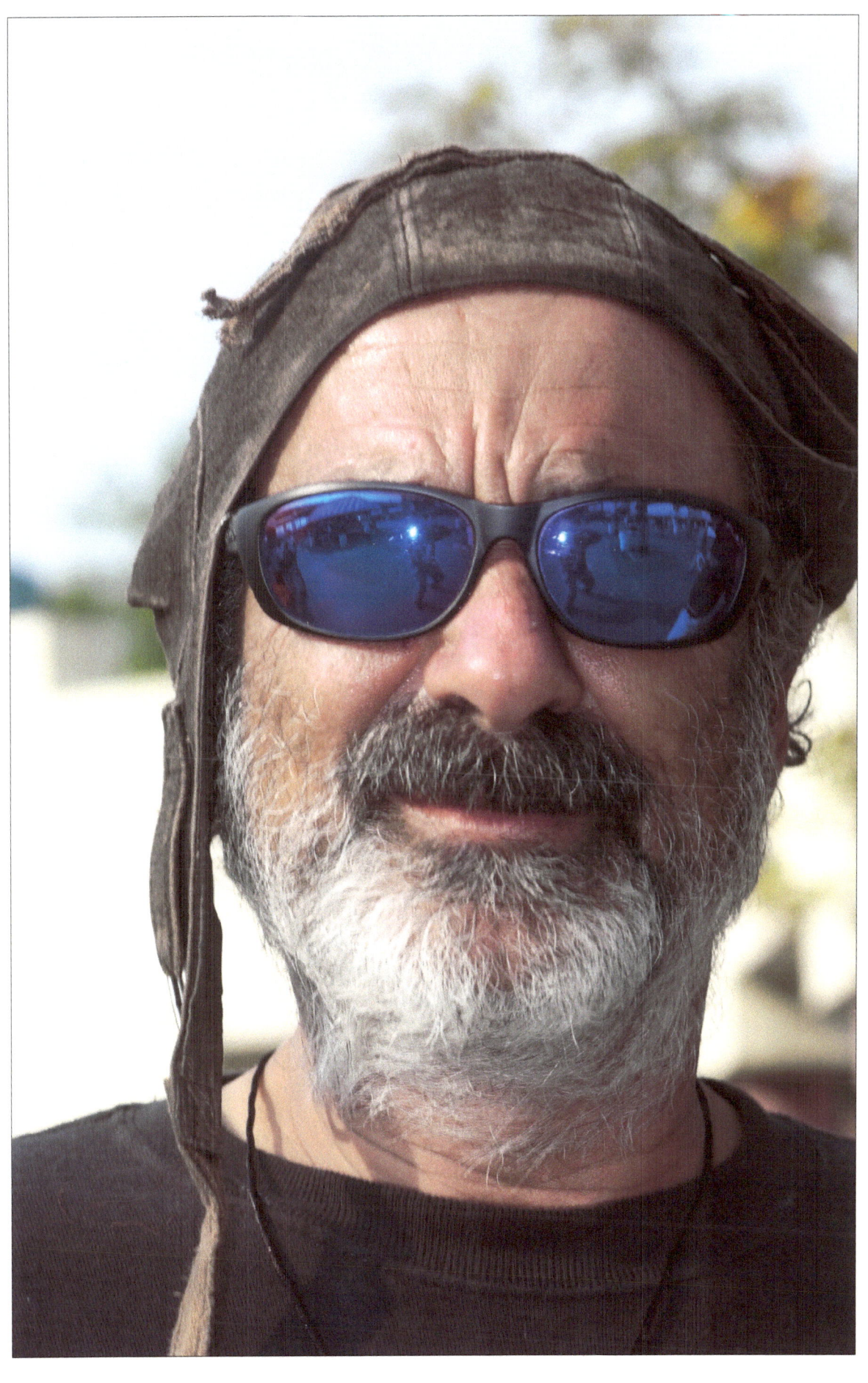

Then she said…

"Why do you need

more than one bike?"

—Author unknown

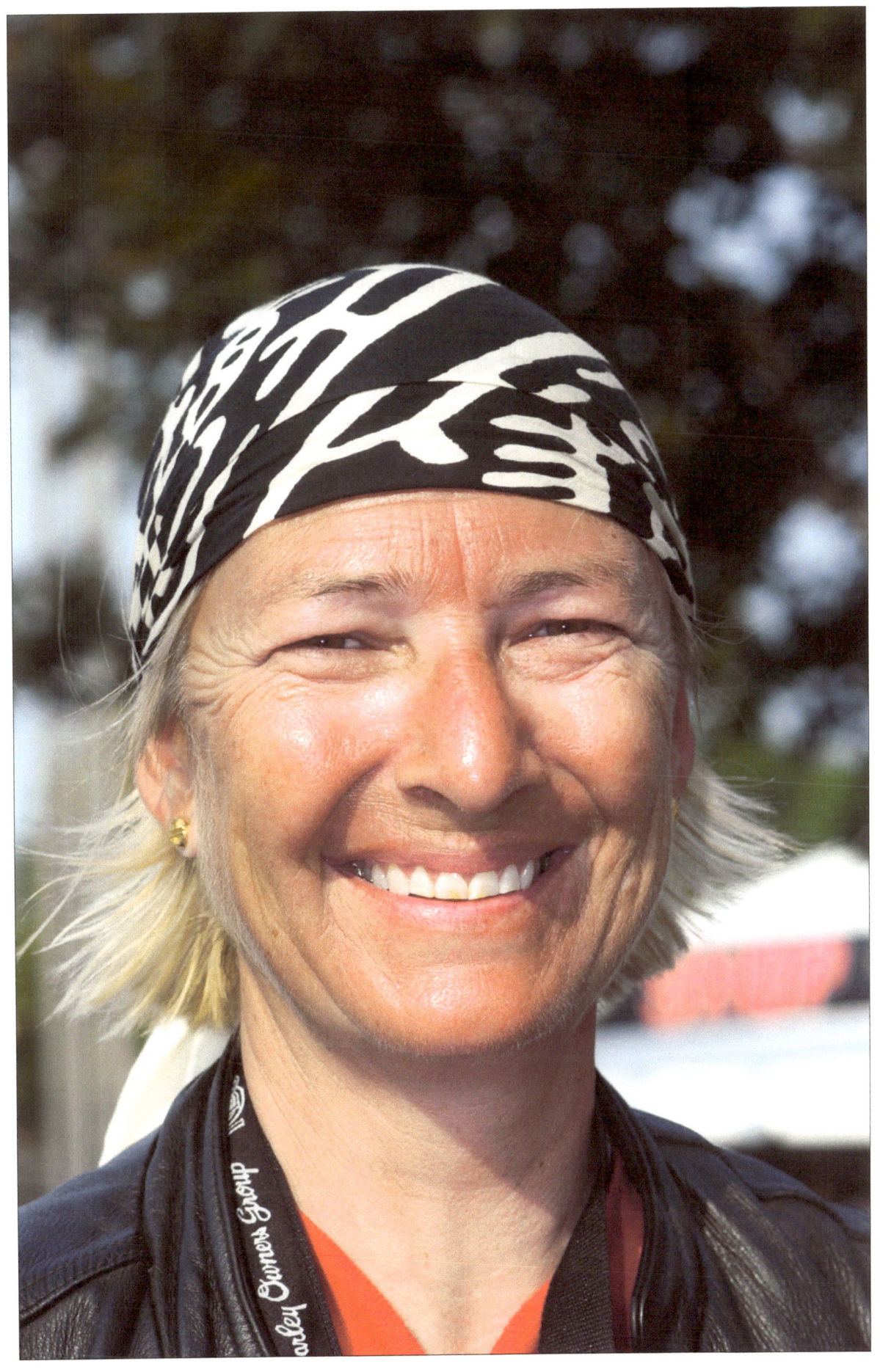

I don't think a woman riding a motorcycle thinks of herself as doing

something that has sex appeal.

I think she's trying to replicate for herself

an experience that she sees men having.

—Rachel Kushner

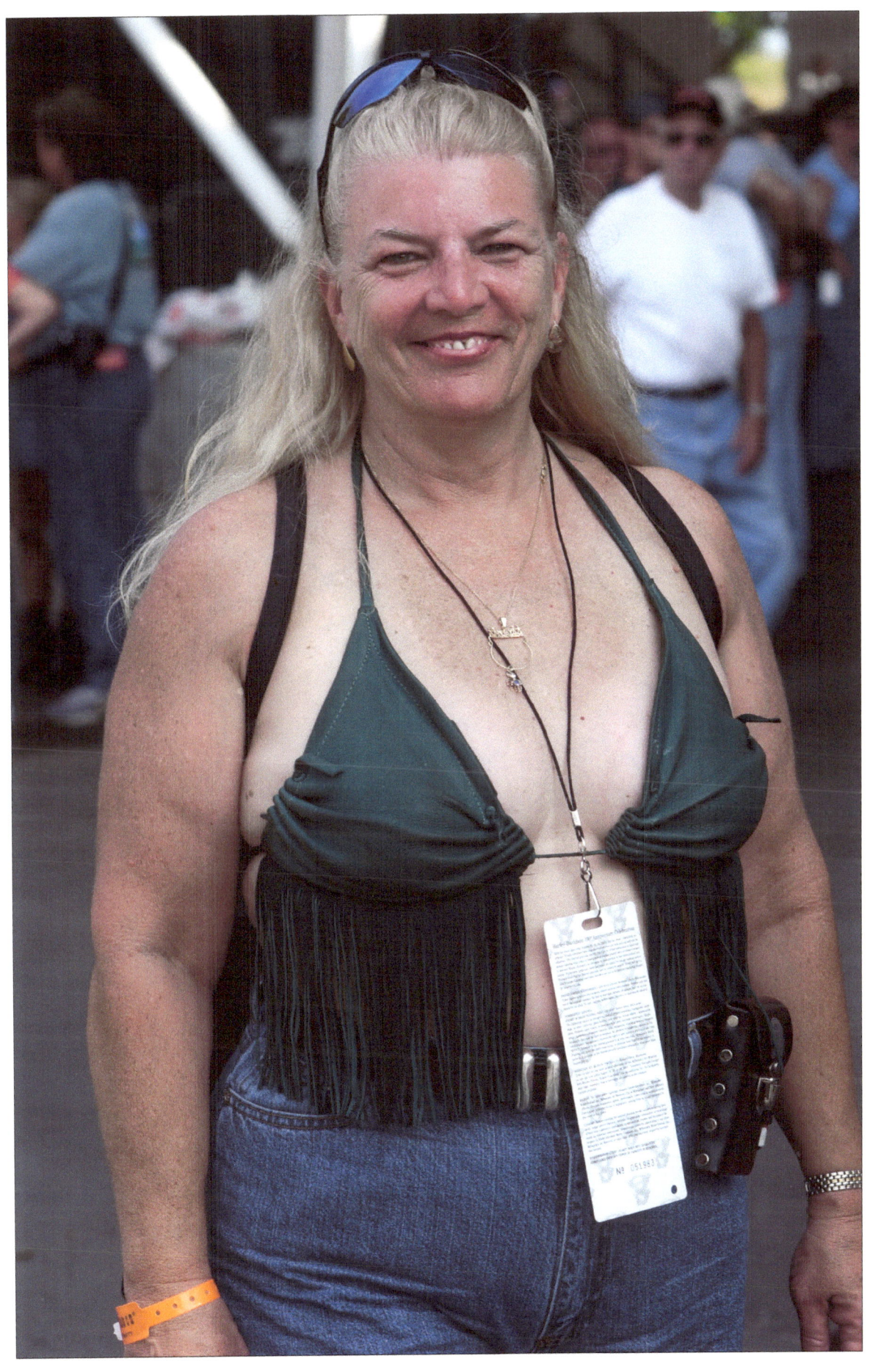

FACES OF HARLEY

If you want to get somewhere before sundown,

you can't stop at every tavern.

—Author unknown

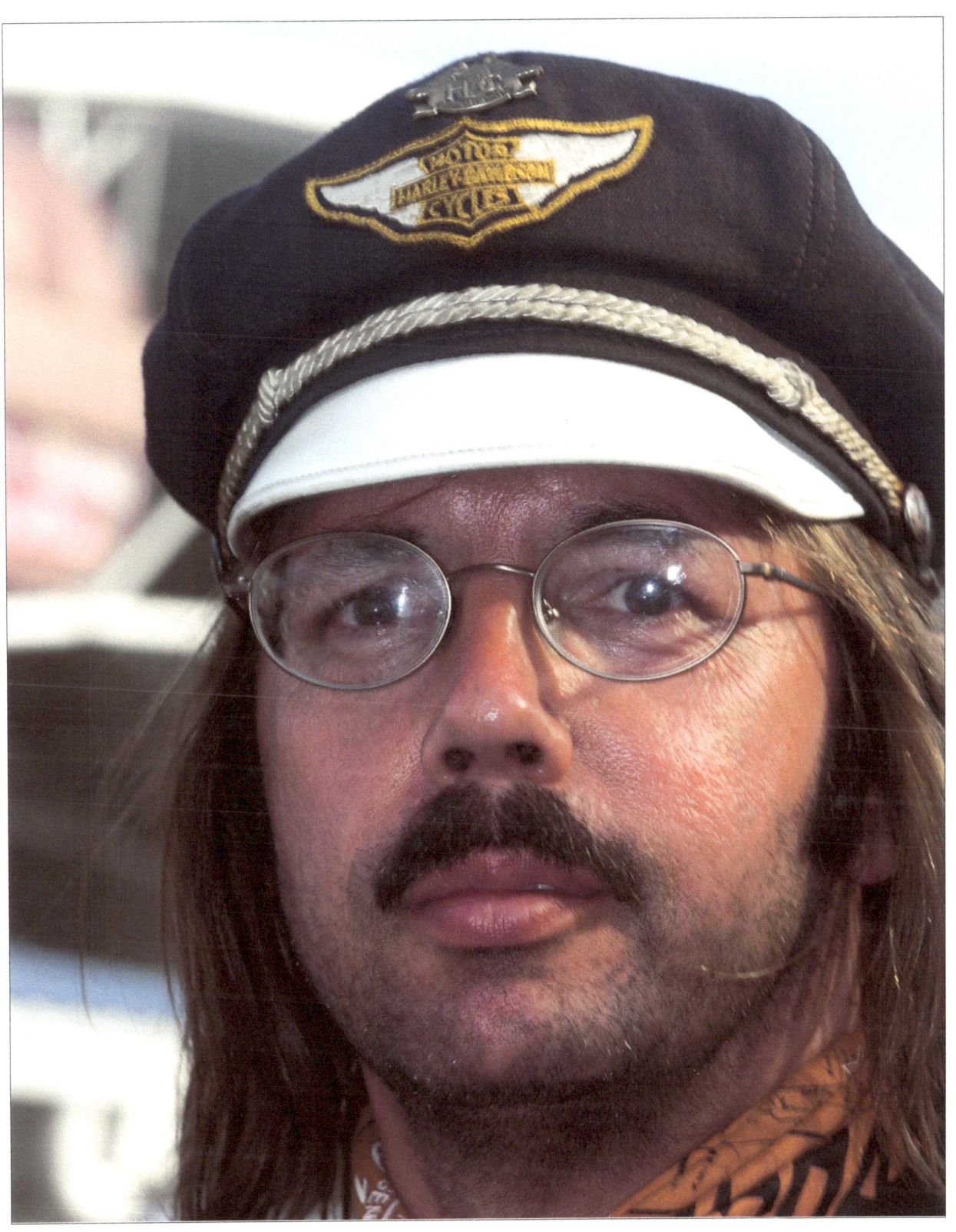

Love is the feeling you get

when you like something as much

as your motorcycle.

—Hunter S. Thompson

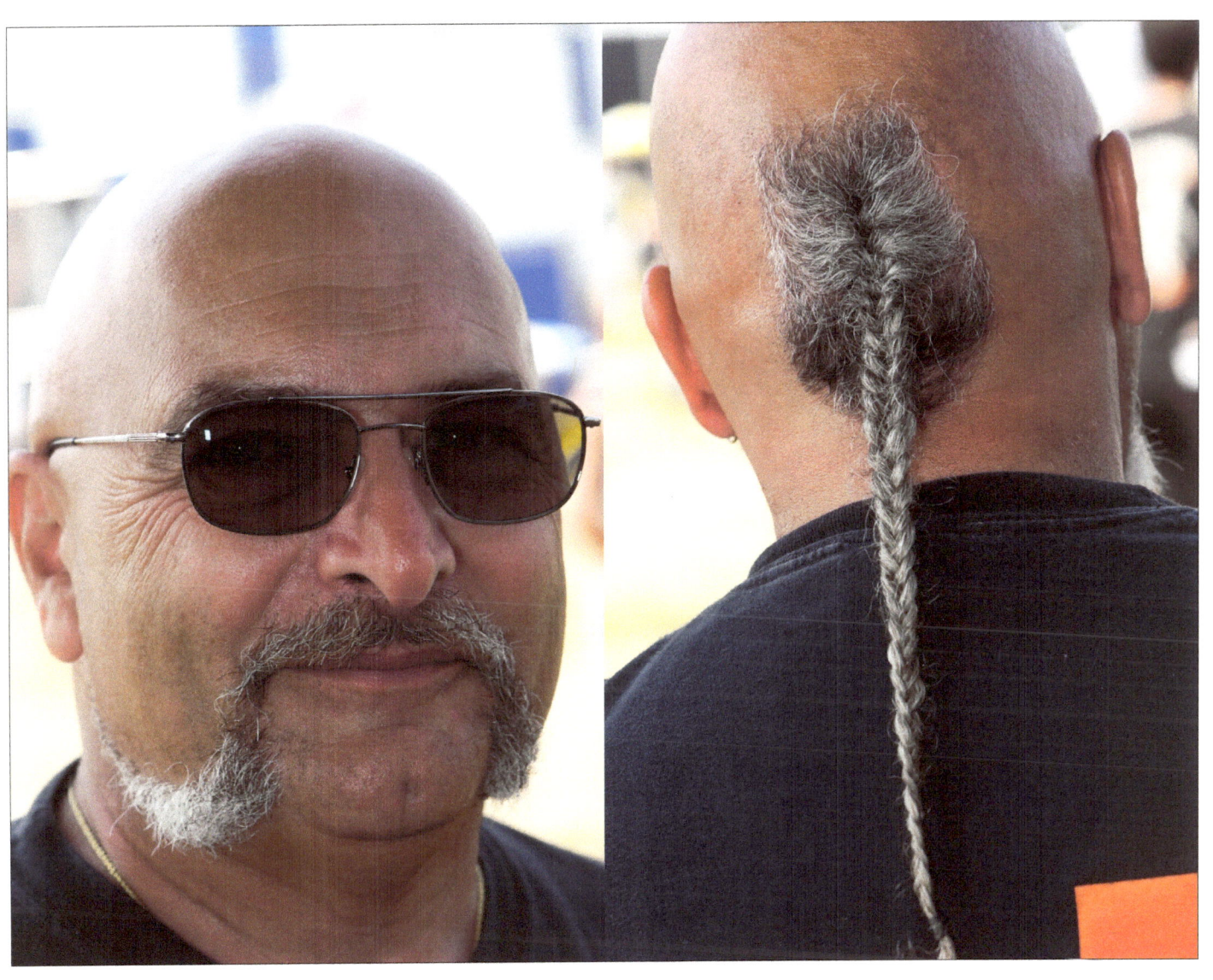

FACES OF HARLEY

From a clean shaven, diffident-appearing youngster

    newly graduated from

        the Art Center College of Design in Pasadena, CA,

Davidson has transformed himself

    into the grinning, macho, bearded icon

        of motorcycledom known to Harley devotees as

            "Willie G."
                    —James Auer

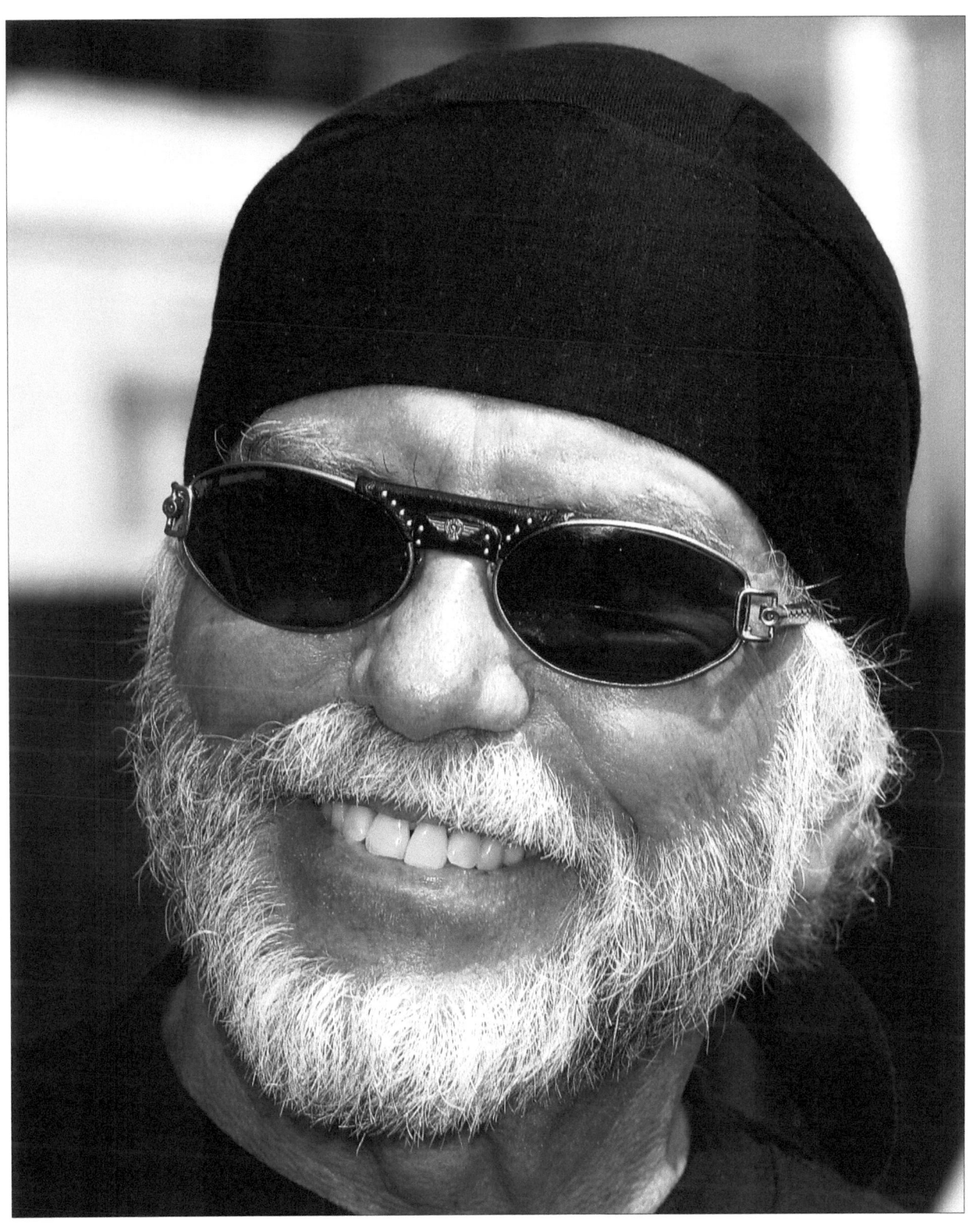

Only a biker knows

why a dog sticks his head

out a car window.

—Author Unknown

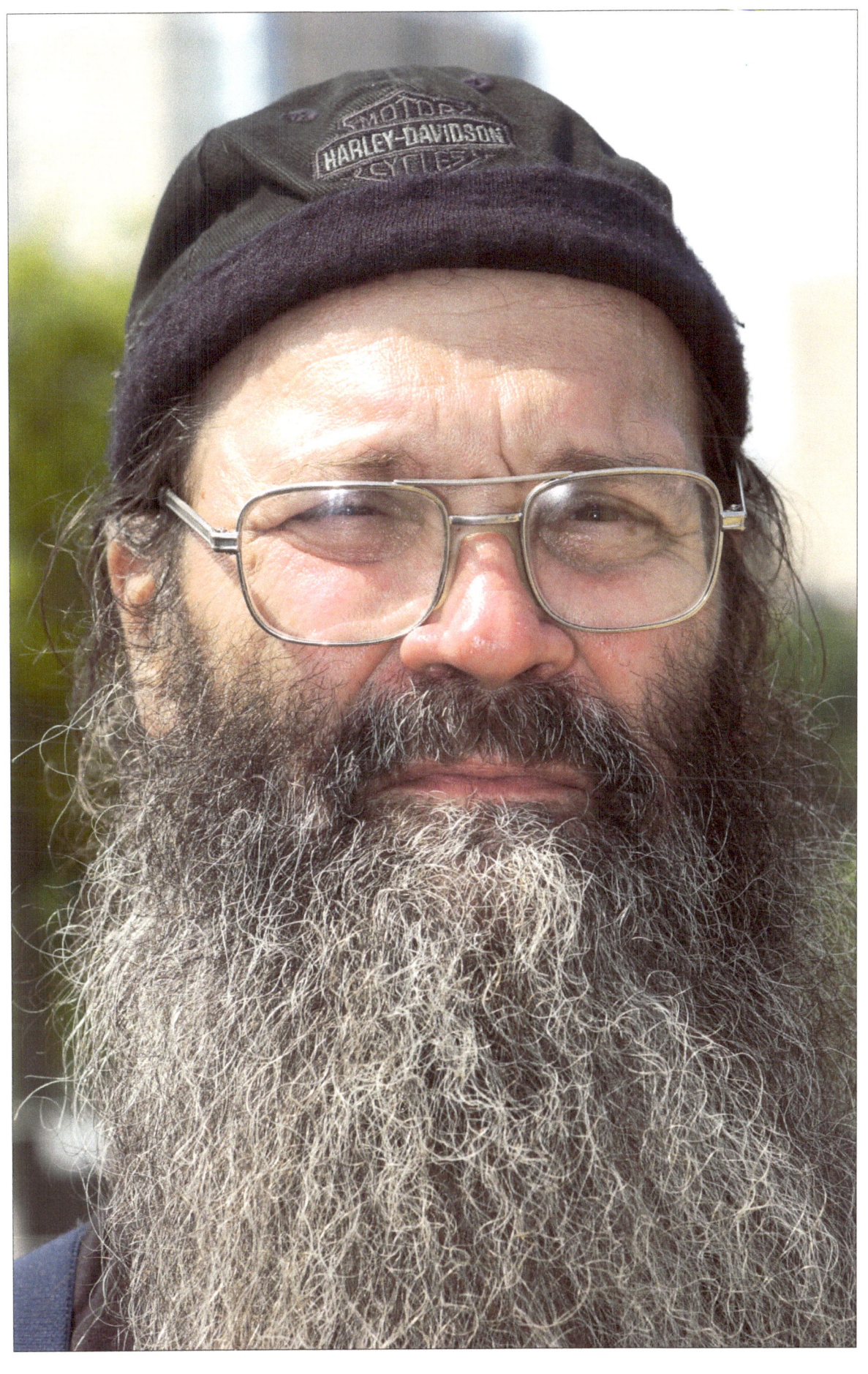

Sometimes the best communication

happens when you're

on separate bikes.

—Author unknown

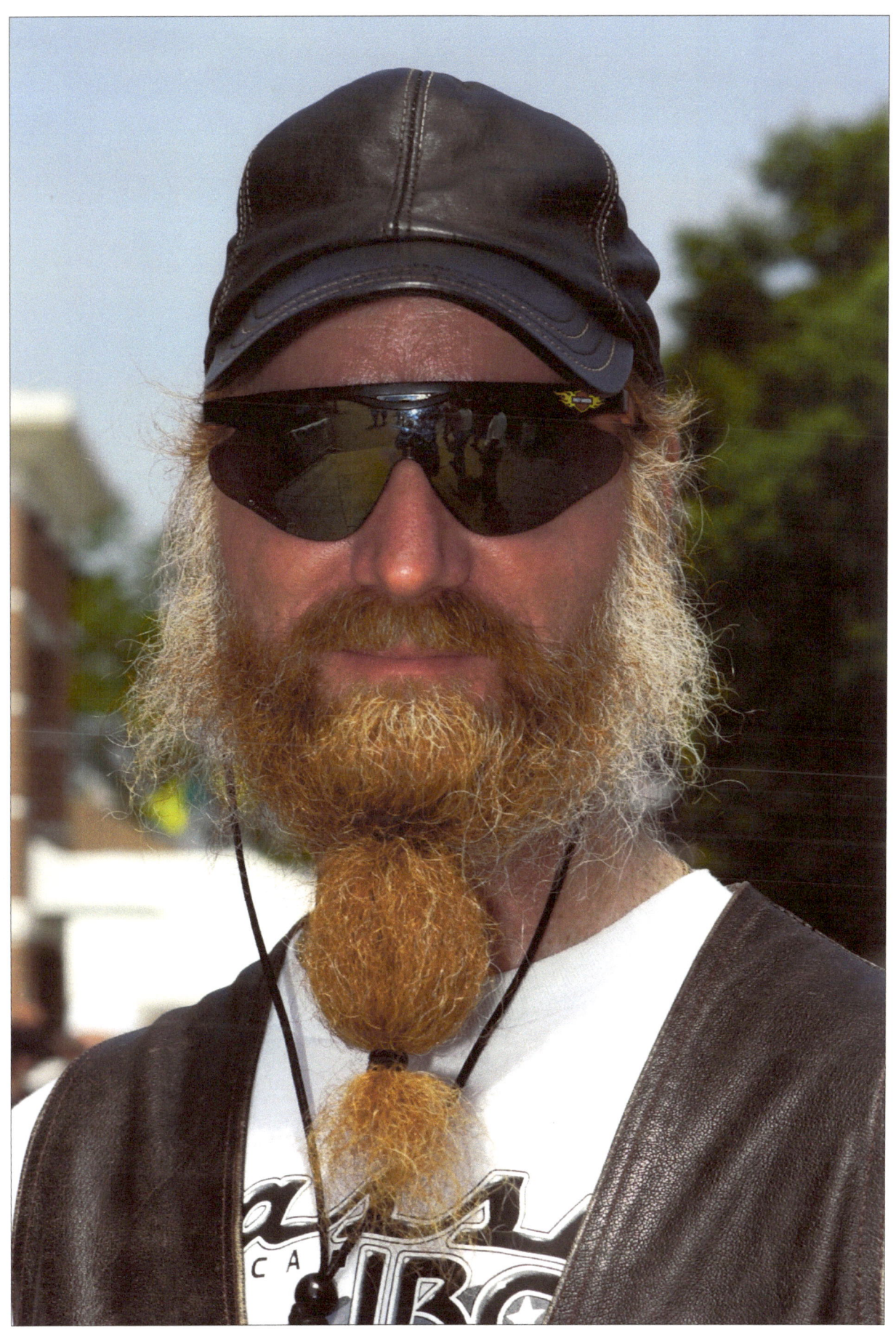

Told him it was me or the motorcycle…

That was the longest wheelie

up the street I'd ever seen!

—Author unknown

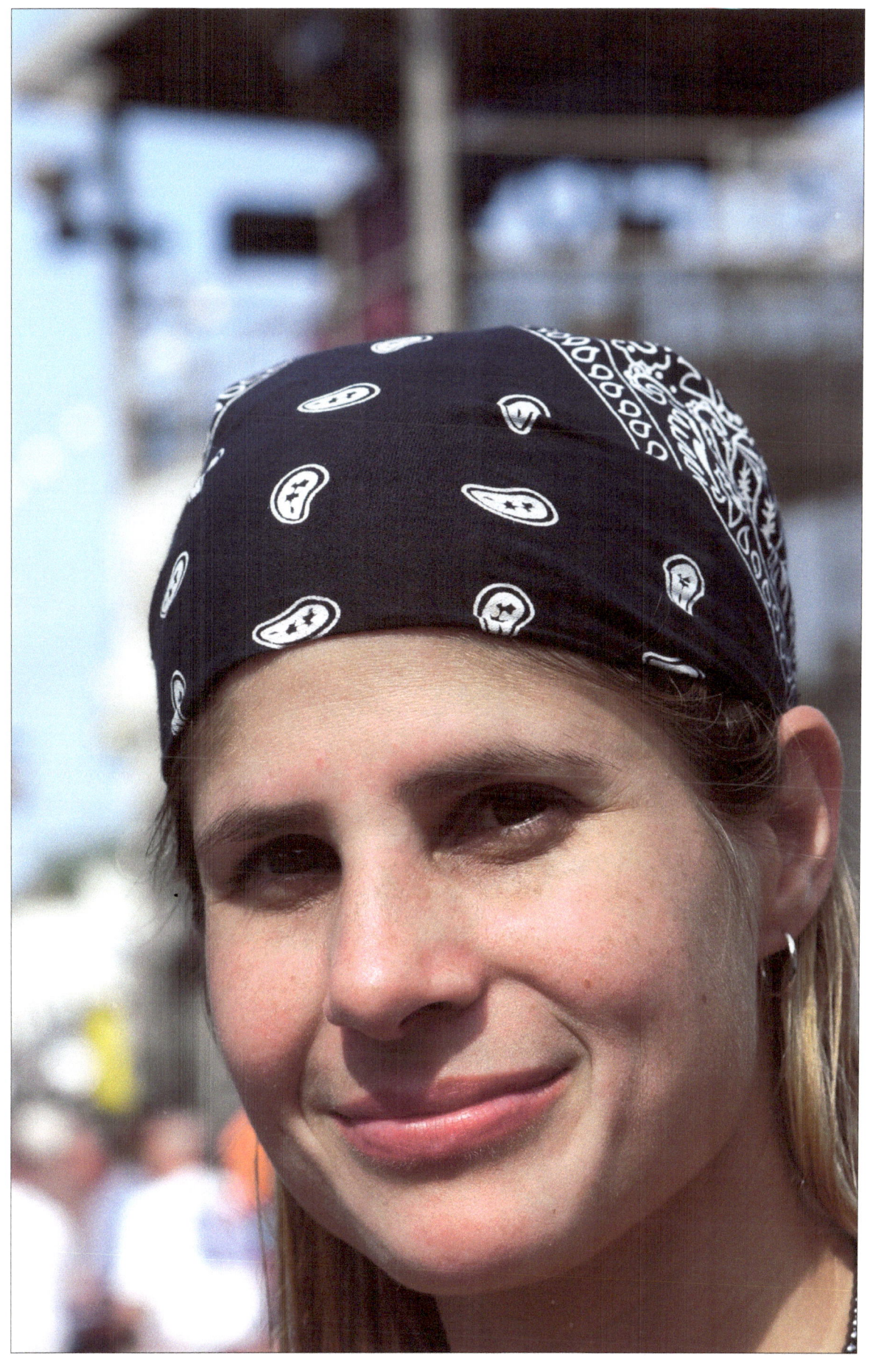

My favorite accessory is

my motorcycle.

—Author unknown

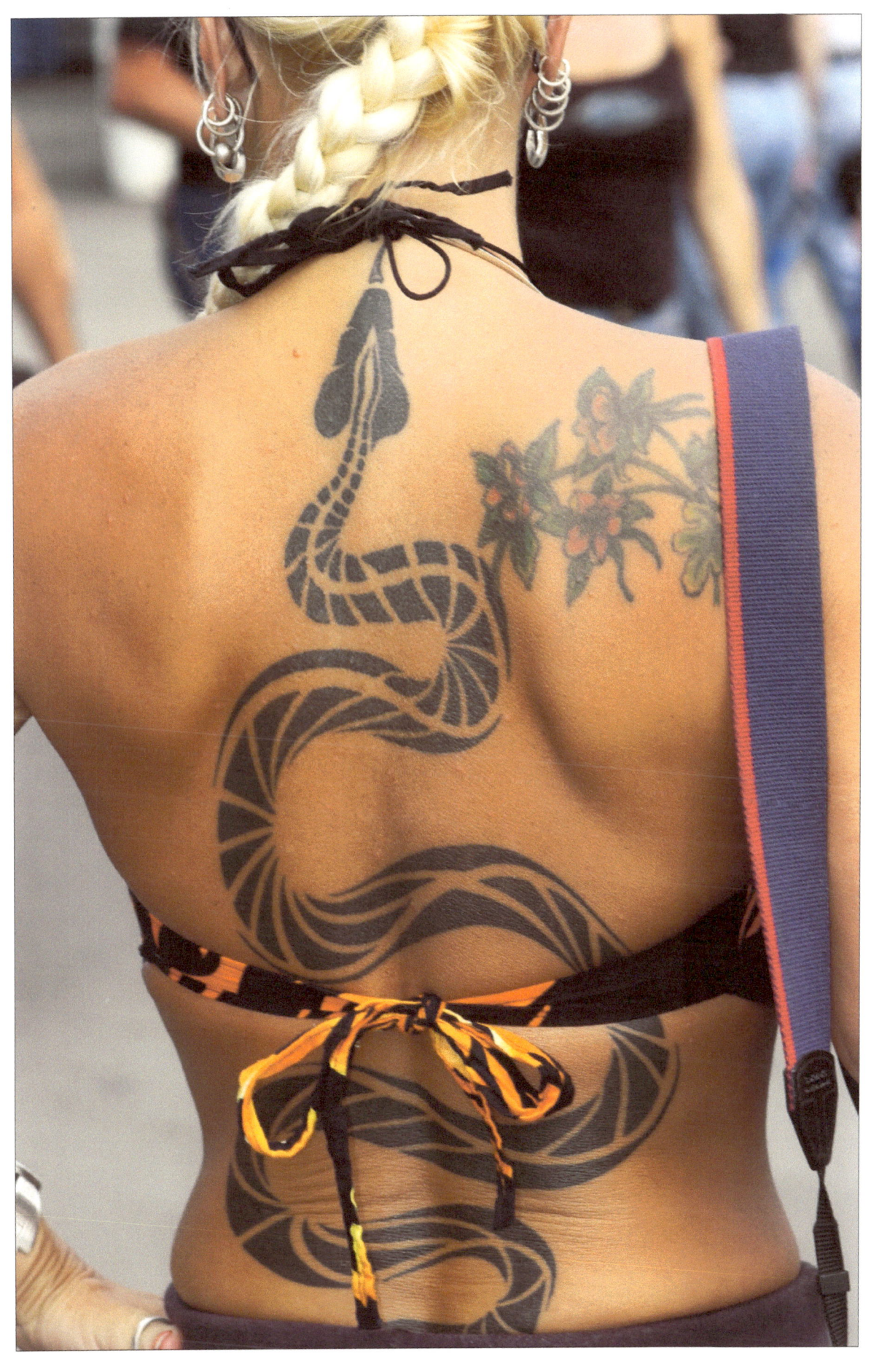

If you really want to know what's going on,

watch what's happening

at least five vehicles ahead.

—Author unknown

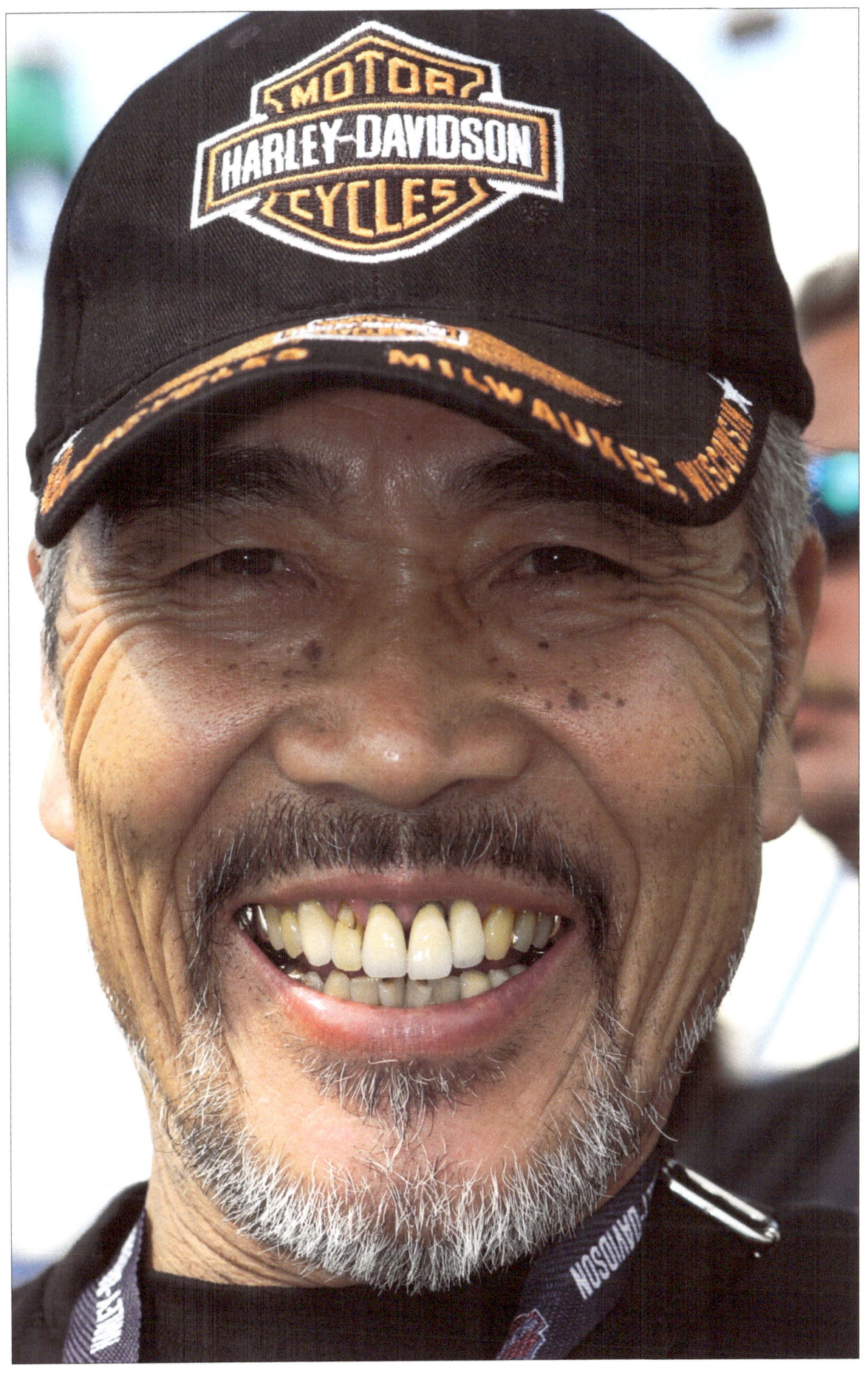

FACES OF HARLEY

I have crashed on a motorcycle

that was going at 140 mph,

so I know what it feels like.

—Rachel Kushner

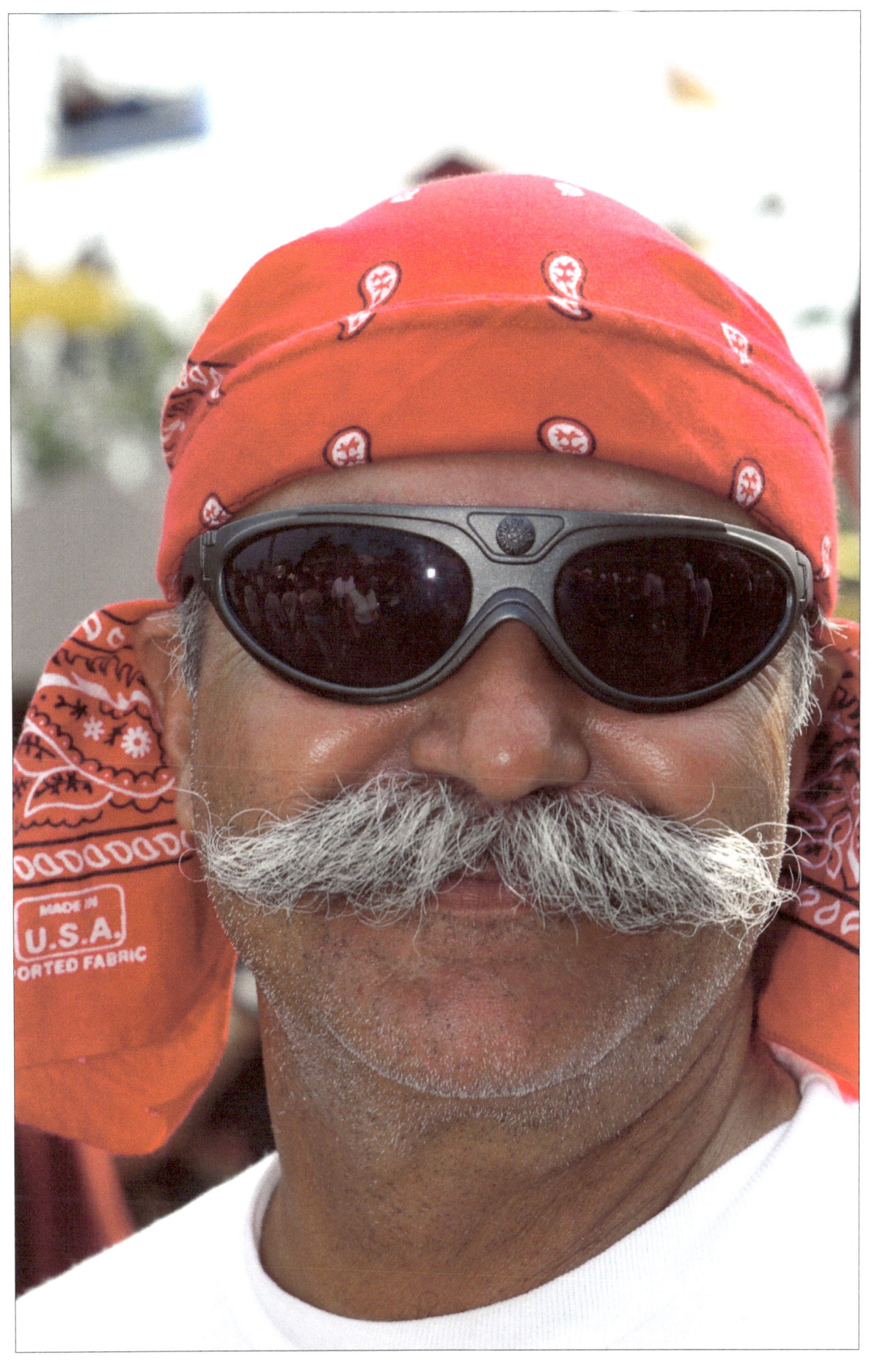

There are those who have crashed and

there are those who will crash.

—Author unknown

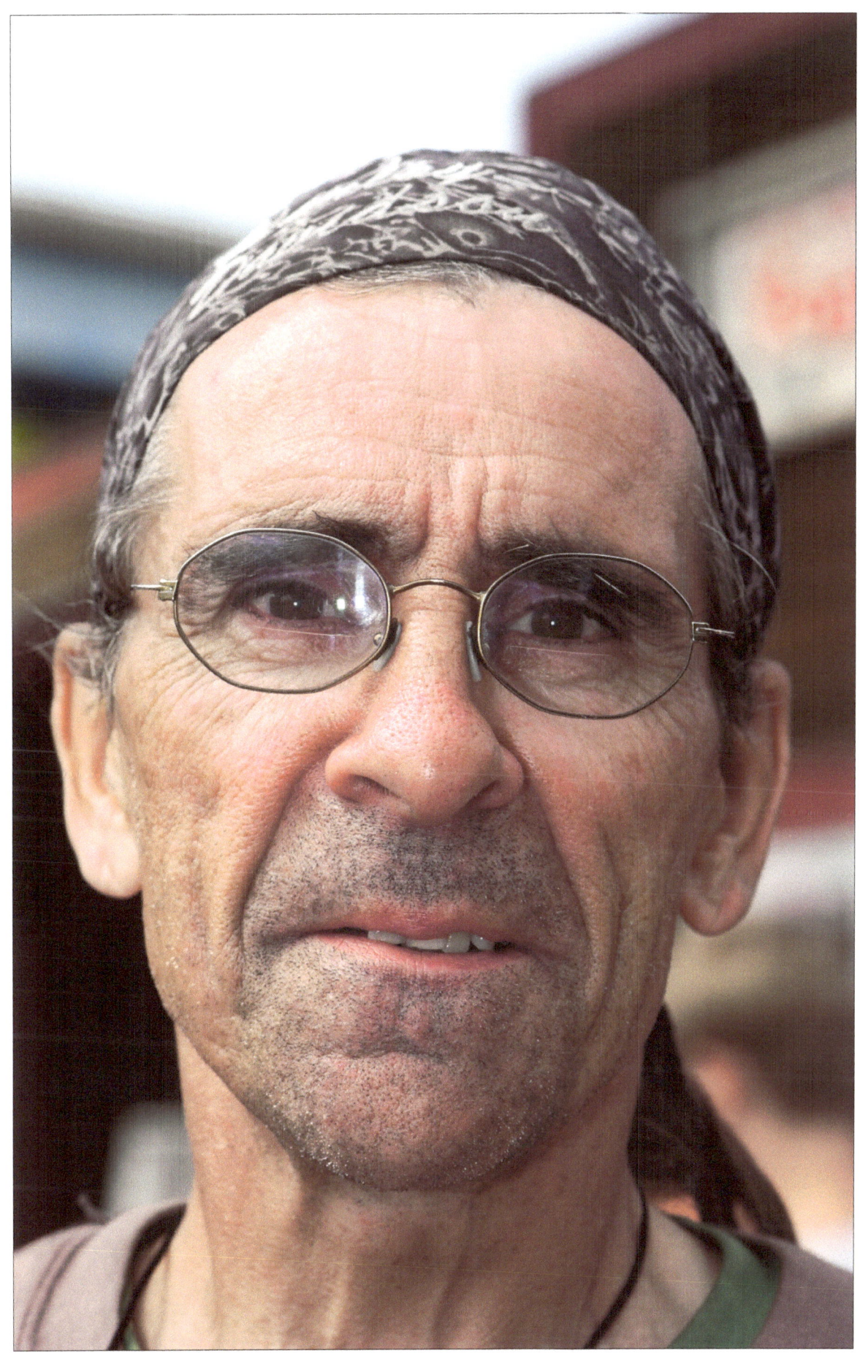

A zest for living must include

a willingness to die.

—R.A. Heinlein

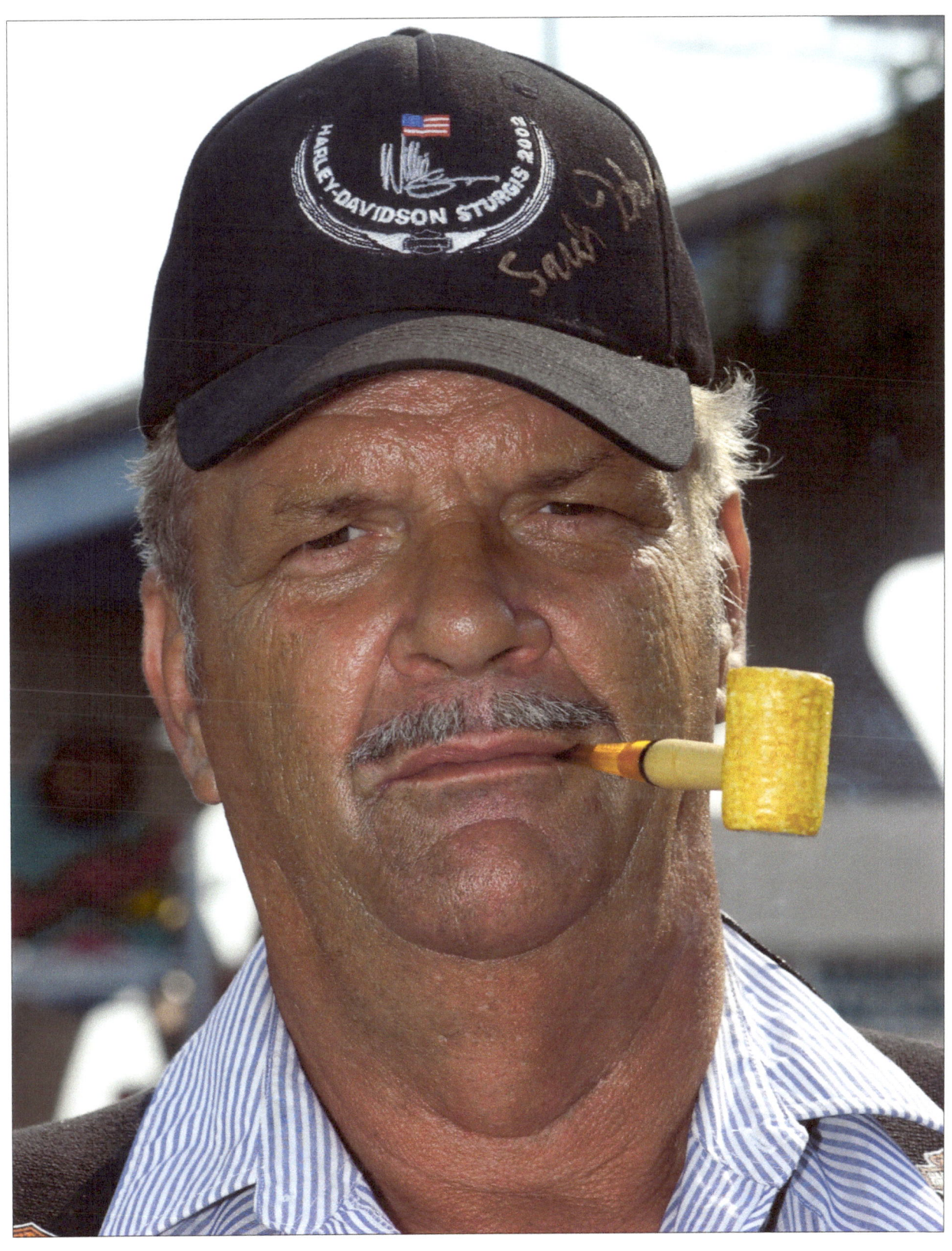

A lot of people are crazy, cruel and negative.

They got a little too much time on their hands to discuss everybody else.

I have a limited amount of energy to blow in a day.

I'd rather read something that I like or watch a program I enjoy or…

ride my damn motorcycle...

—Queen Latifah

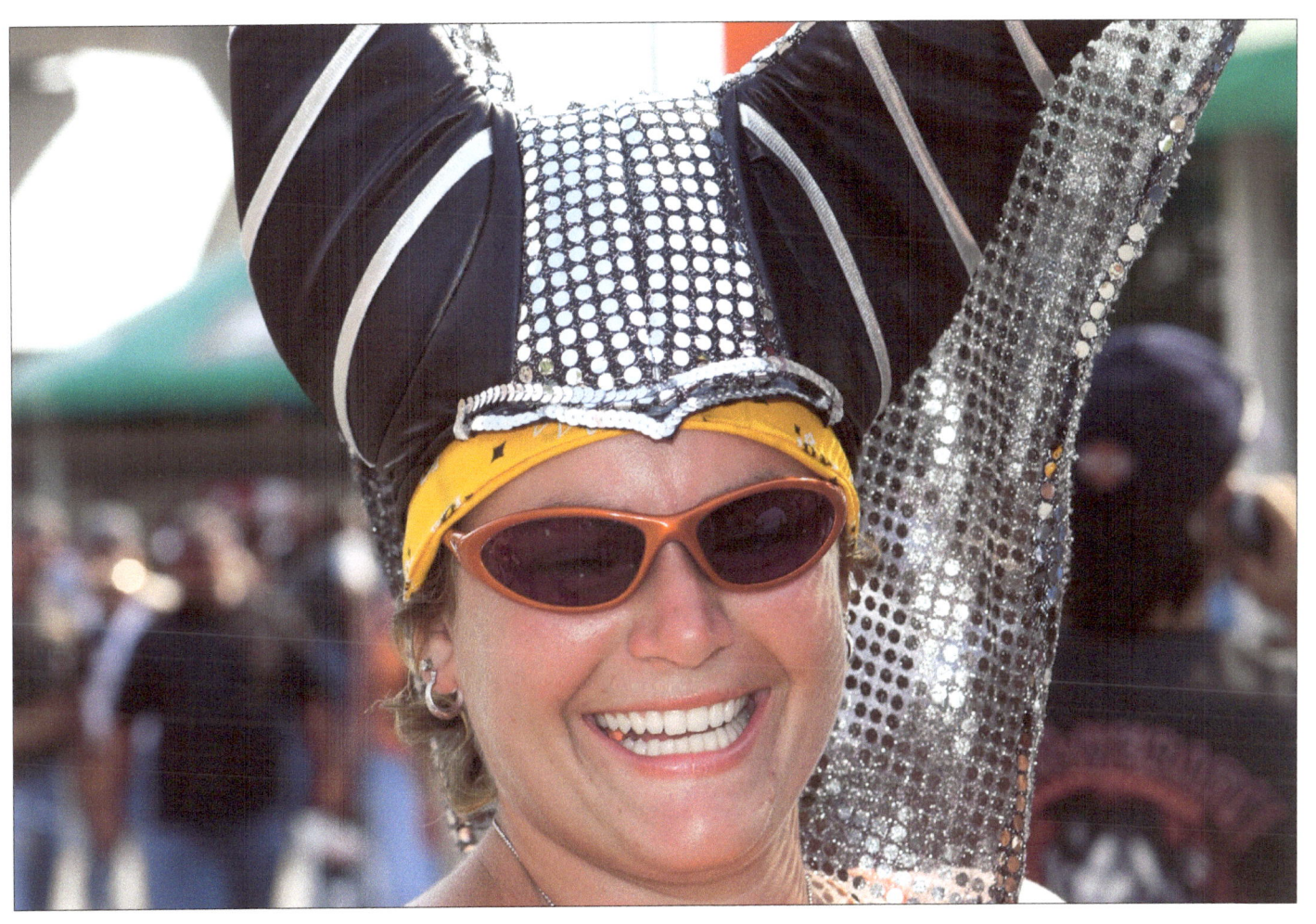

Who said diamonds are

a girl's best friend?

—Author unknown

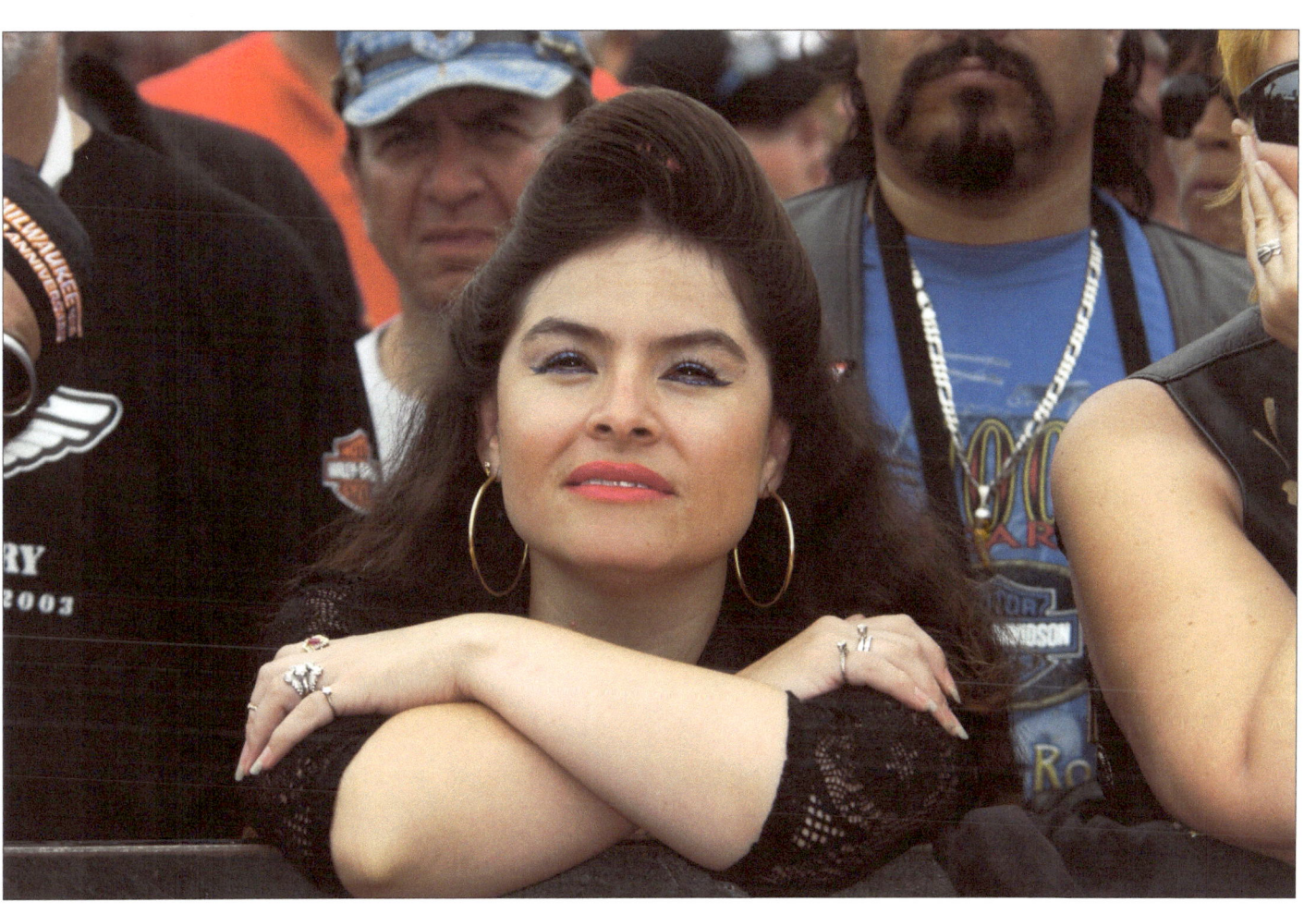

FACES OF HARLEY

The most important thing is to have a good

relationship with the bike…you have to understand

what she wants. I think of a motorcycle as a woman, and I know that

sounds silly, but it's true.

—Valentino Rossi

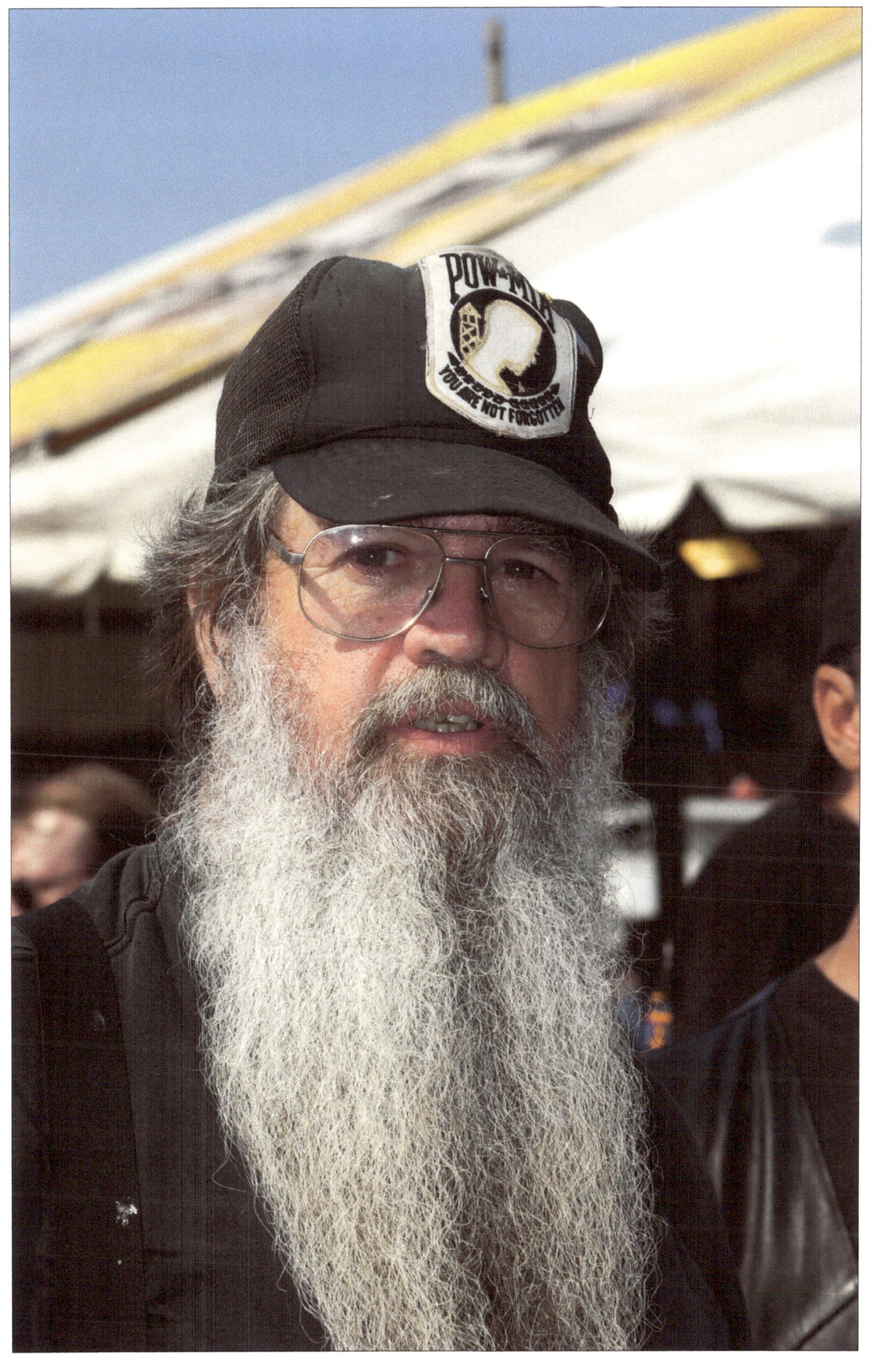

FACES OF HARLEY

I'd rather be riding my motorcycle

thinking about God

than sitting in church

thinking about my motorcycle.

—Anon

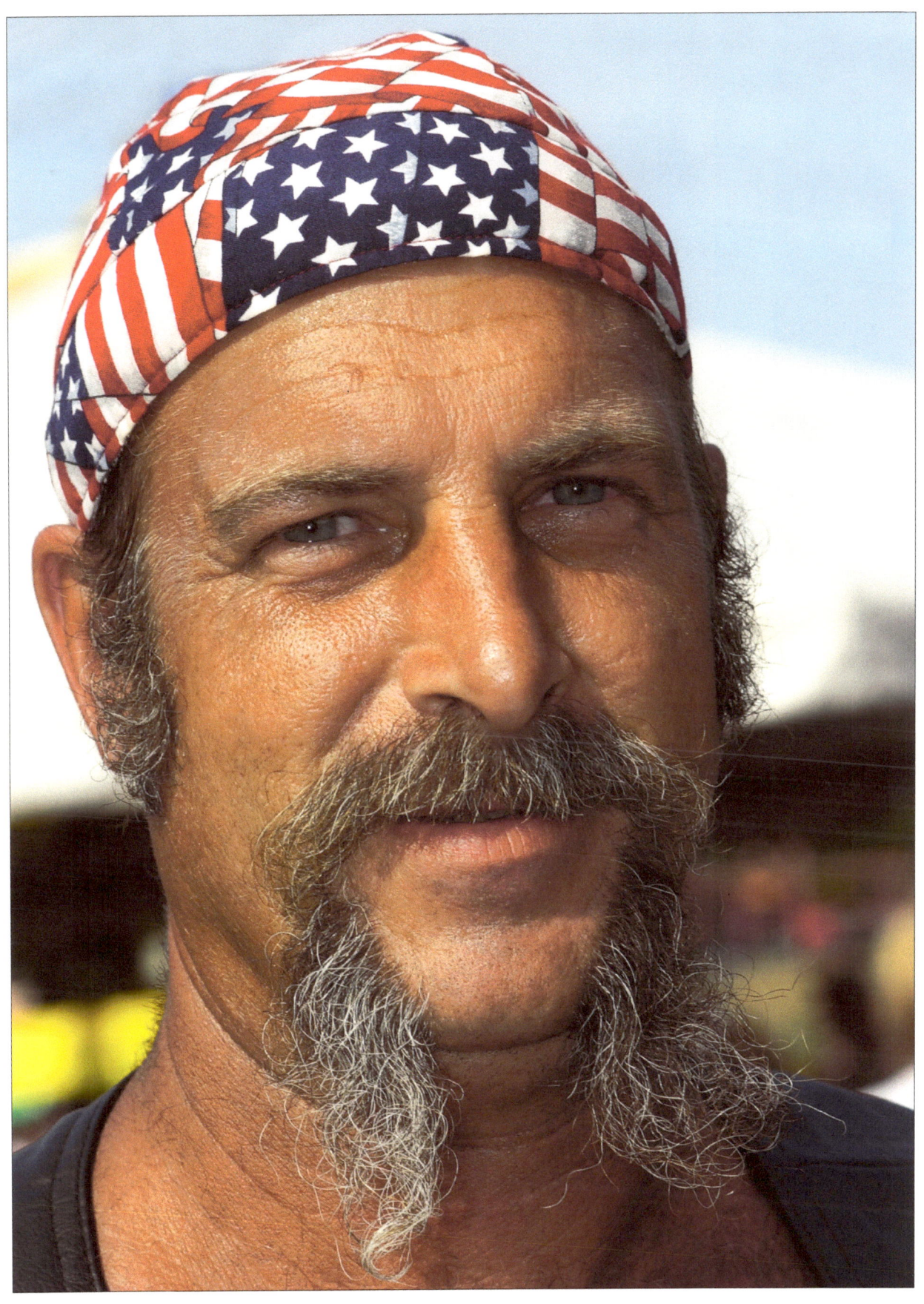

FACES OF HARLEY

"Easy Rider" was never a motorcycle movie to me.

A lot of it was about politically

what was going on in the country.

—Dennis Hopper

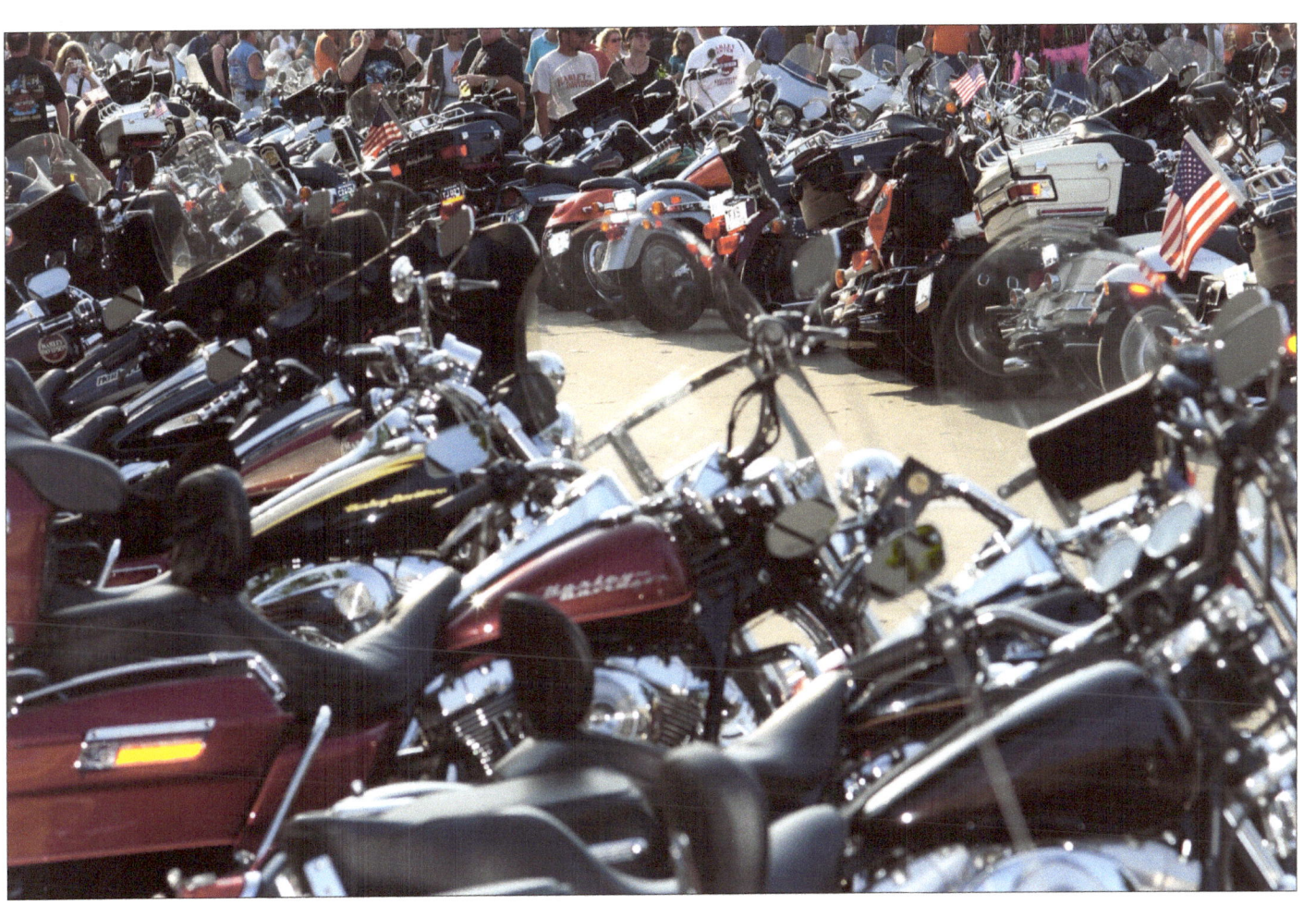

The best alarm clock is

sunshine on chrome.

—Author Unknown

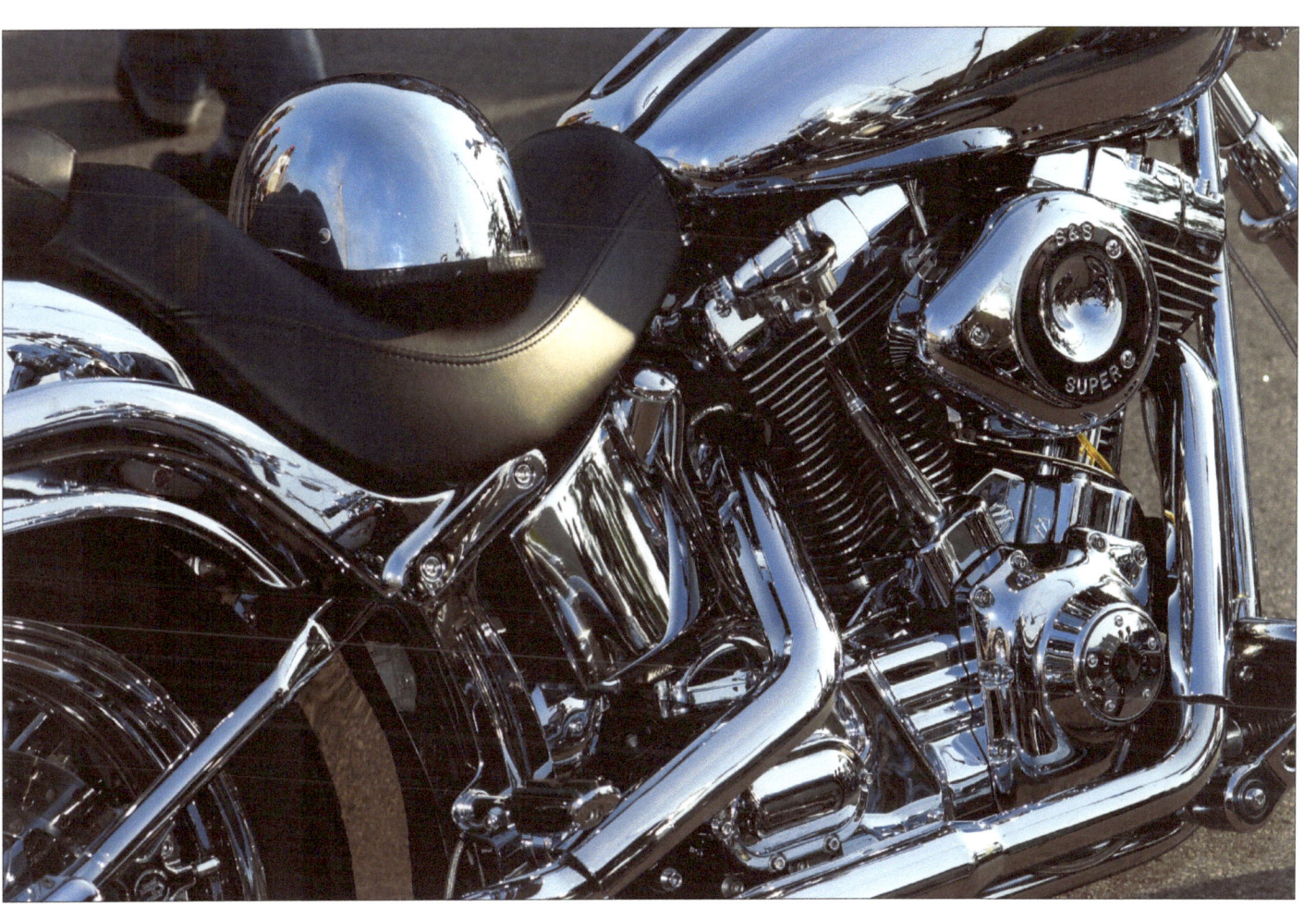

Seen on a motorcycle's rearviews:

"Warning: objects seen in mirror are disappearing rapidly"

—Author unknown

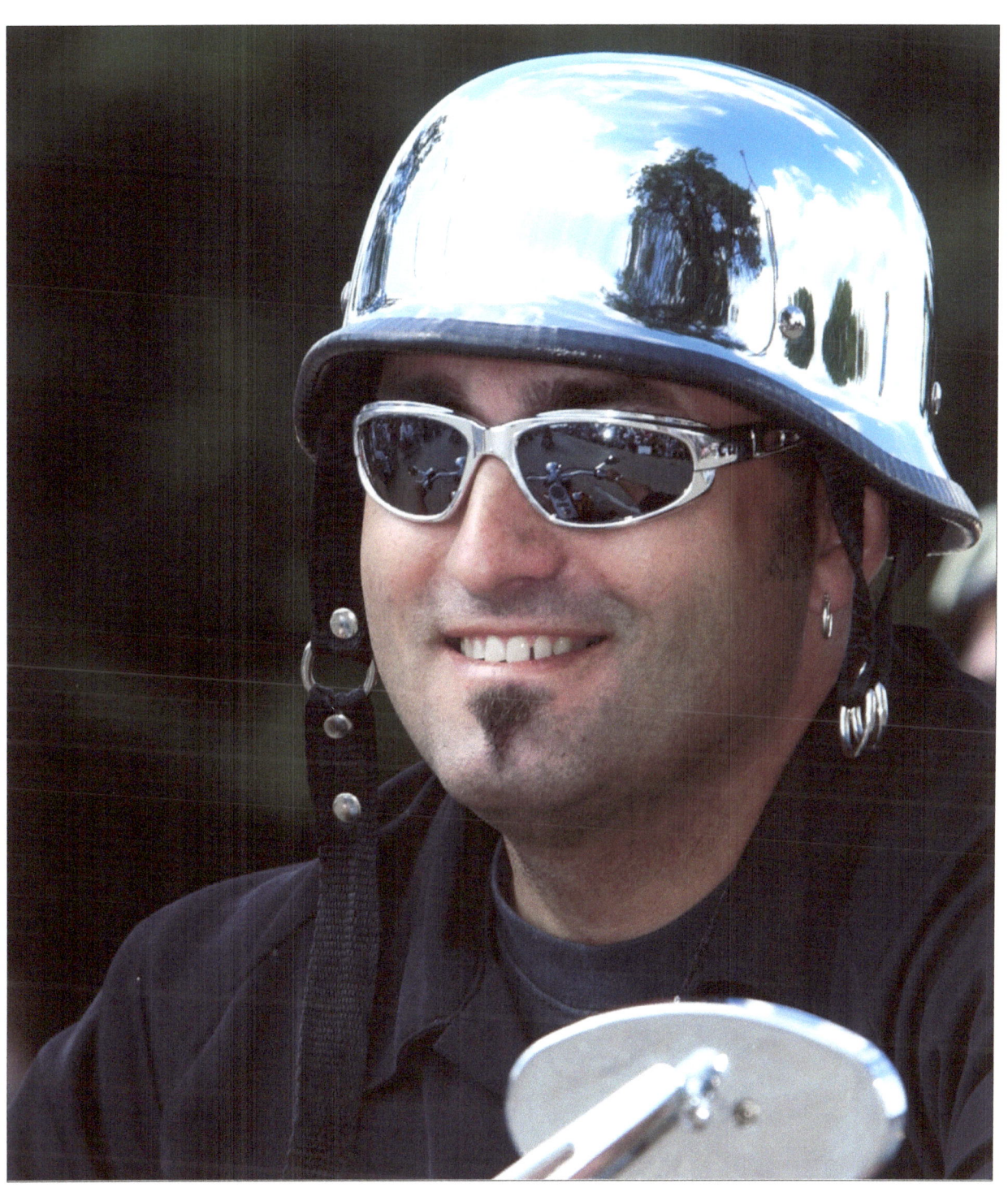

I've spent my entire career on horseback or on a motorcycle.

It boxes you in, the way people perceive you.

I read a lot of scripts.

Most of 'em go to other actors.

—Sam Elliott

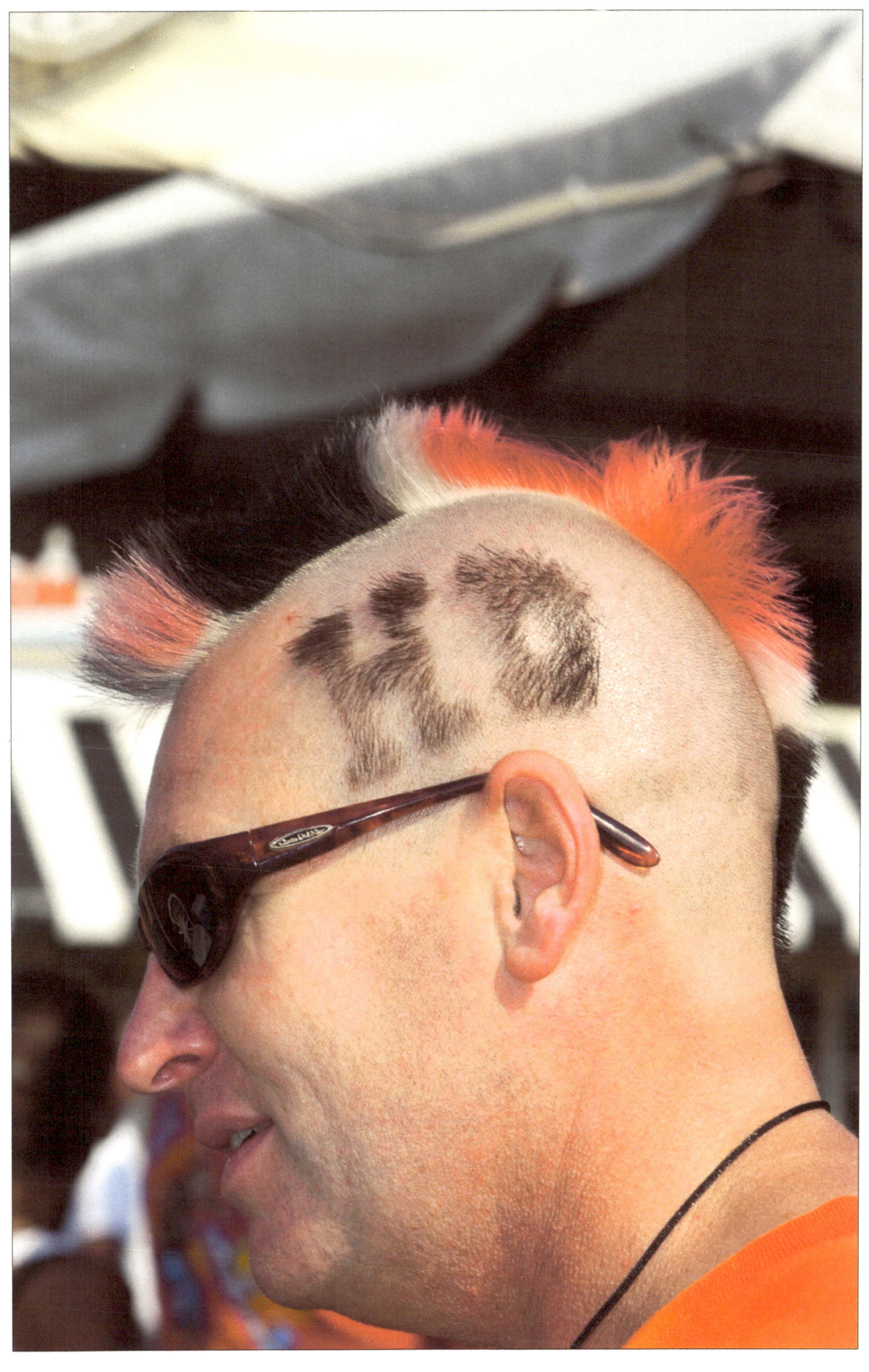

FACES OF HARLEY

Being a biker is more than riding a bike.

You feel it in your heart and in your soul.

—Author unknown

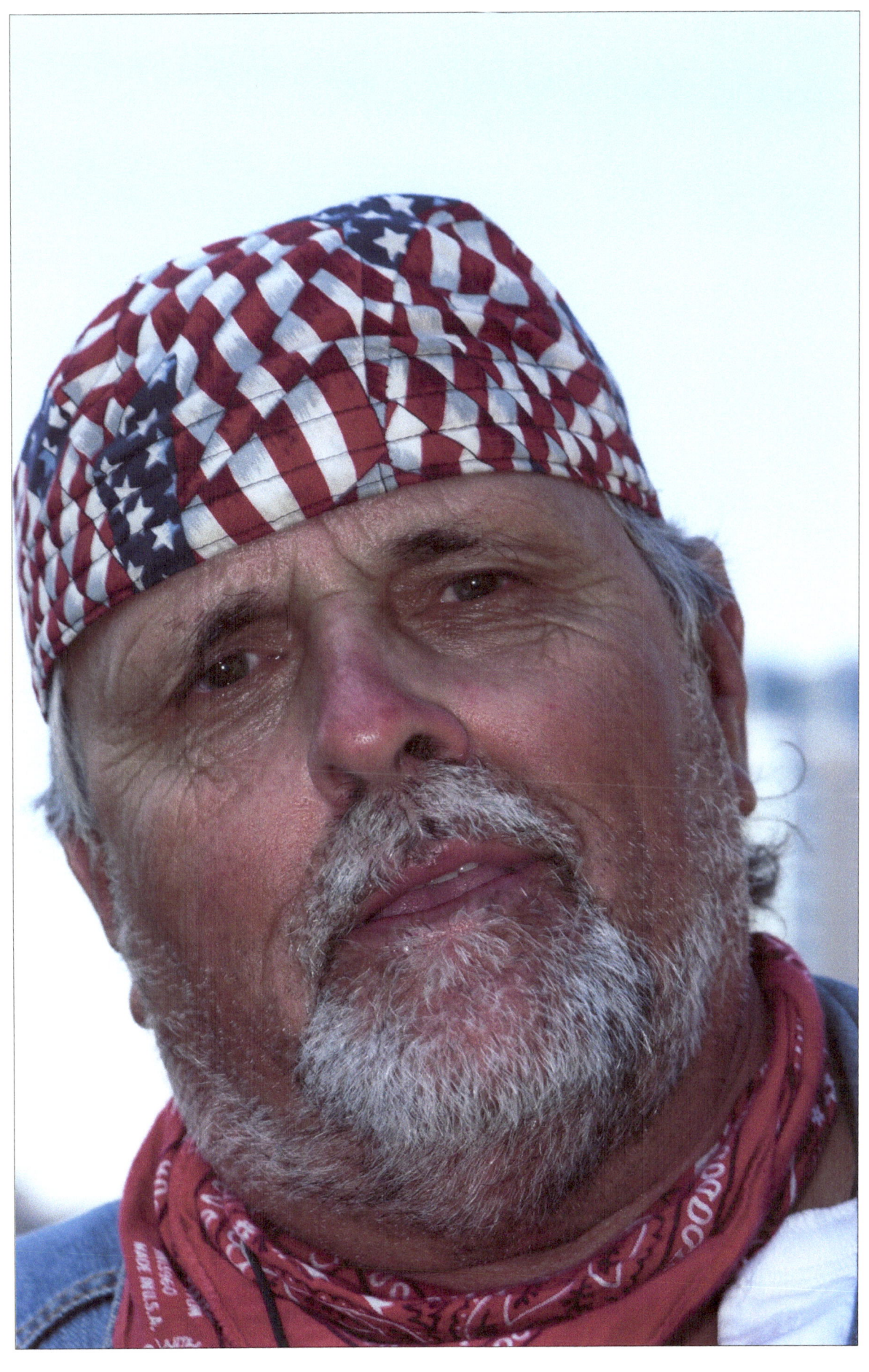

If she chooses a day

on the bike over a

day of shopping…

then you got yourself a

keeper.

—Author unknown

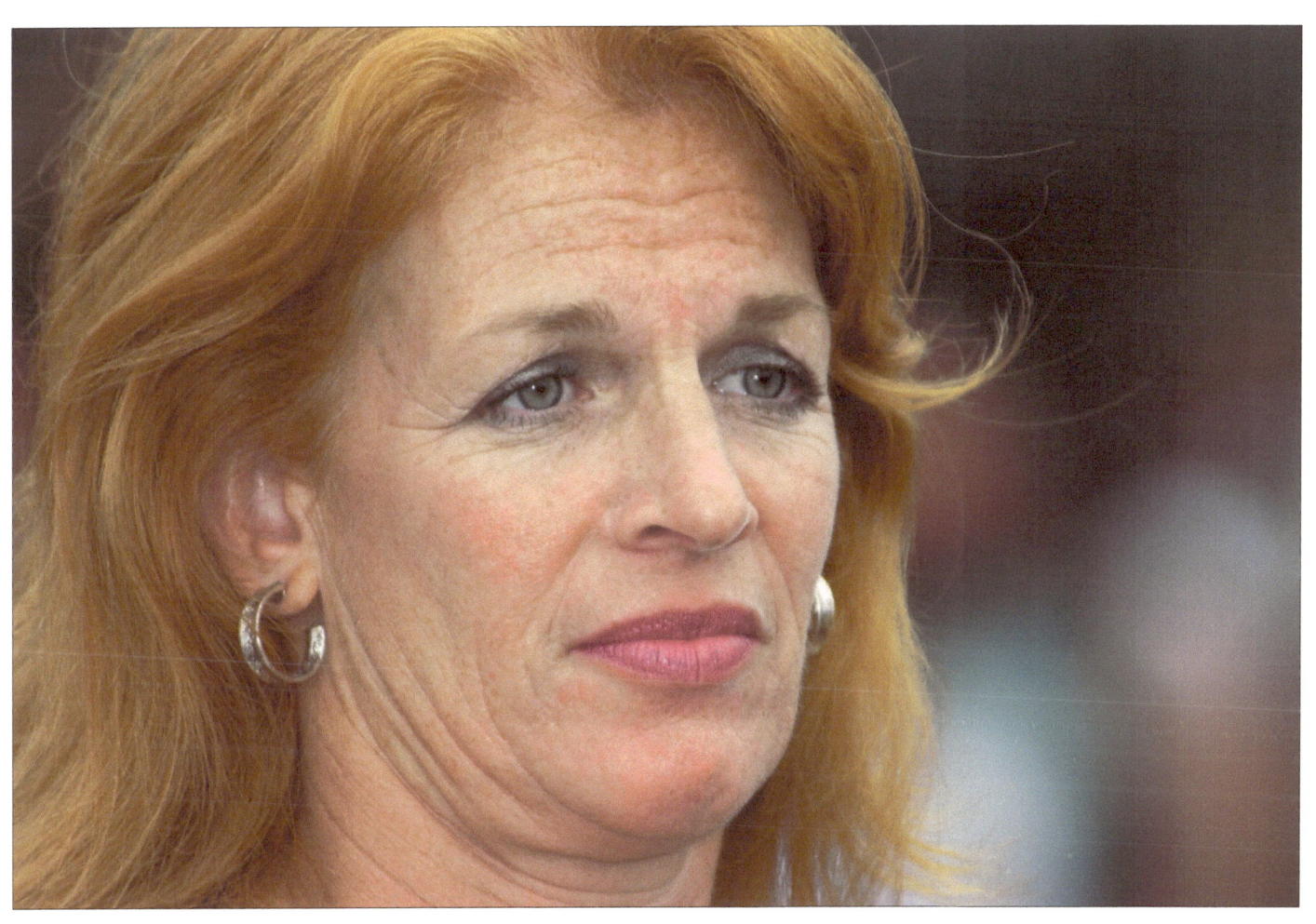

The first time I went to Sturgis,

I remember thinking,

"This motorcycle thing,

this is me."

—Brantley Gilbert

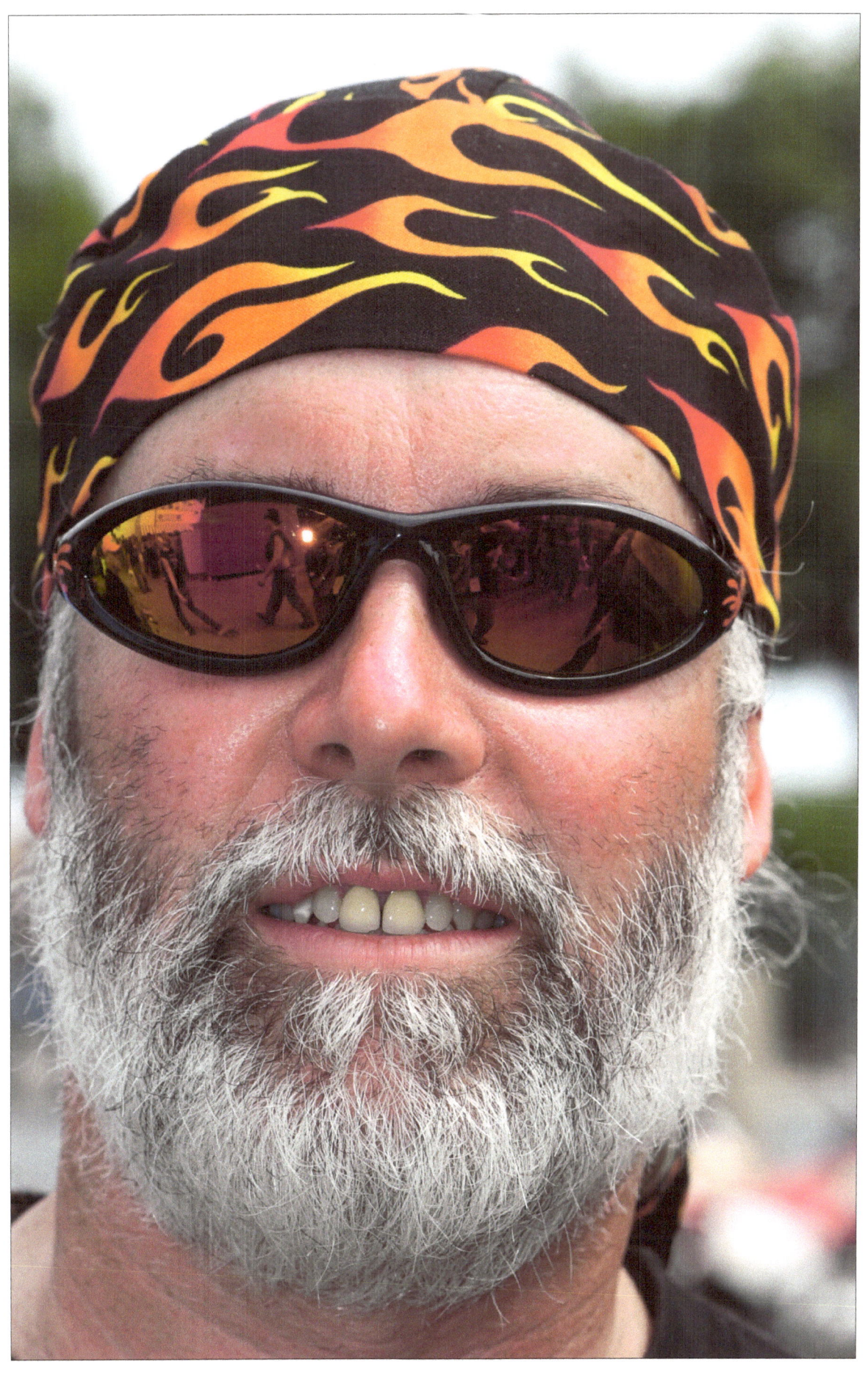

People still say to me,

"What, you still live in Mexico?"

I don't have to go to the United States simply to find work, and

I don't have to stop what I'm doing.

I mean, which Hollywood film beats

"The Motorcycle Diaries?"

—Gael Garcia Bernal

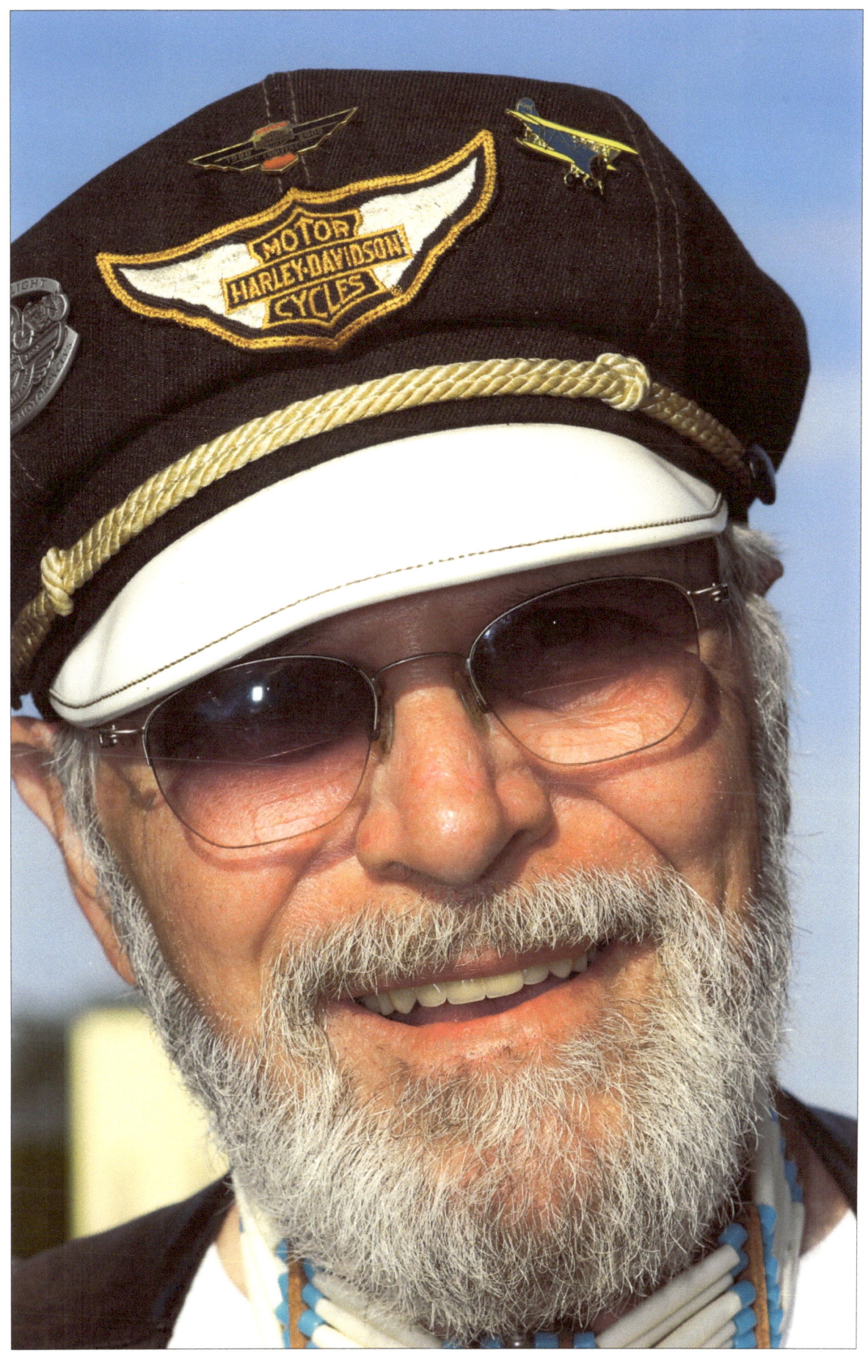

It takes more love

To share the saddle

Than it does

To share the bed

      —Author unknown

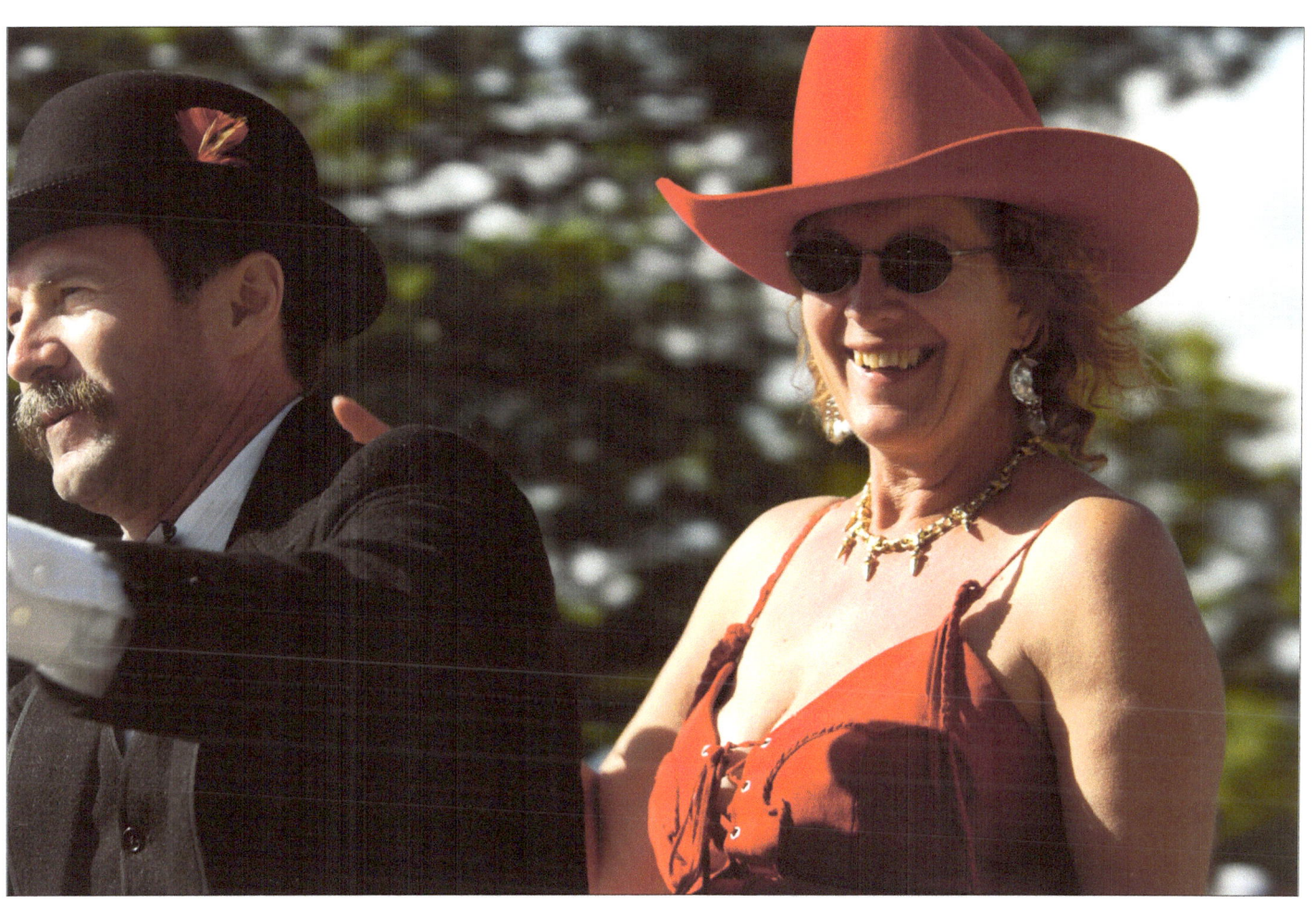

Got a $5 head?

Get a $5 helmet.

—Author unknown

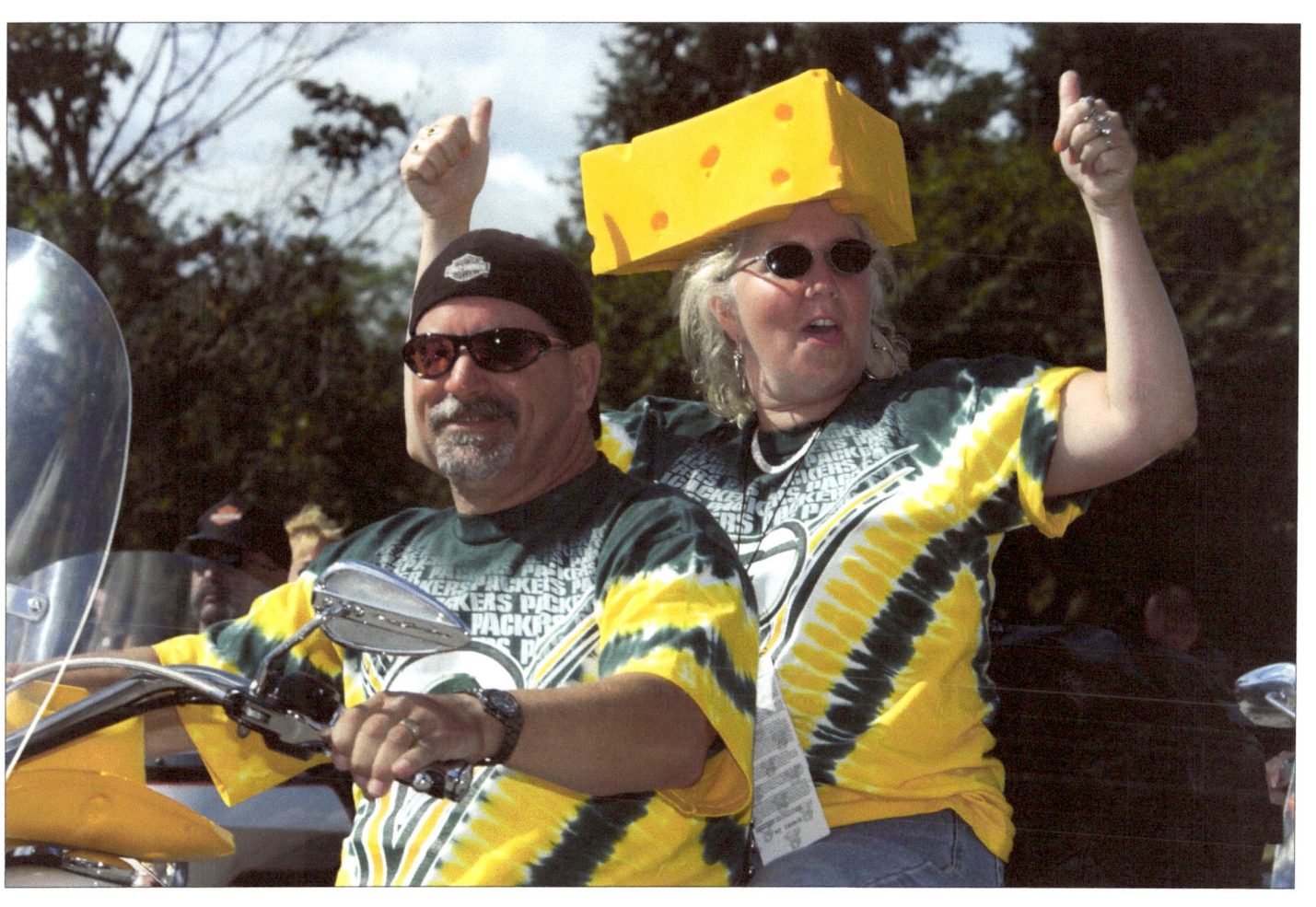

Remember to pay as much attention

    to your partner

as you do

    your carburetor.

        —Author unknown

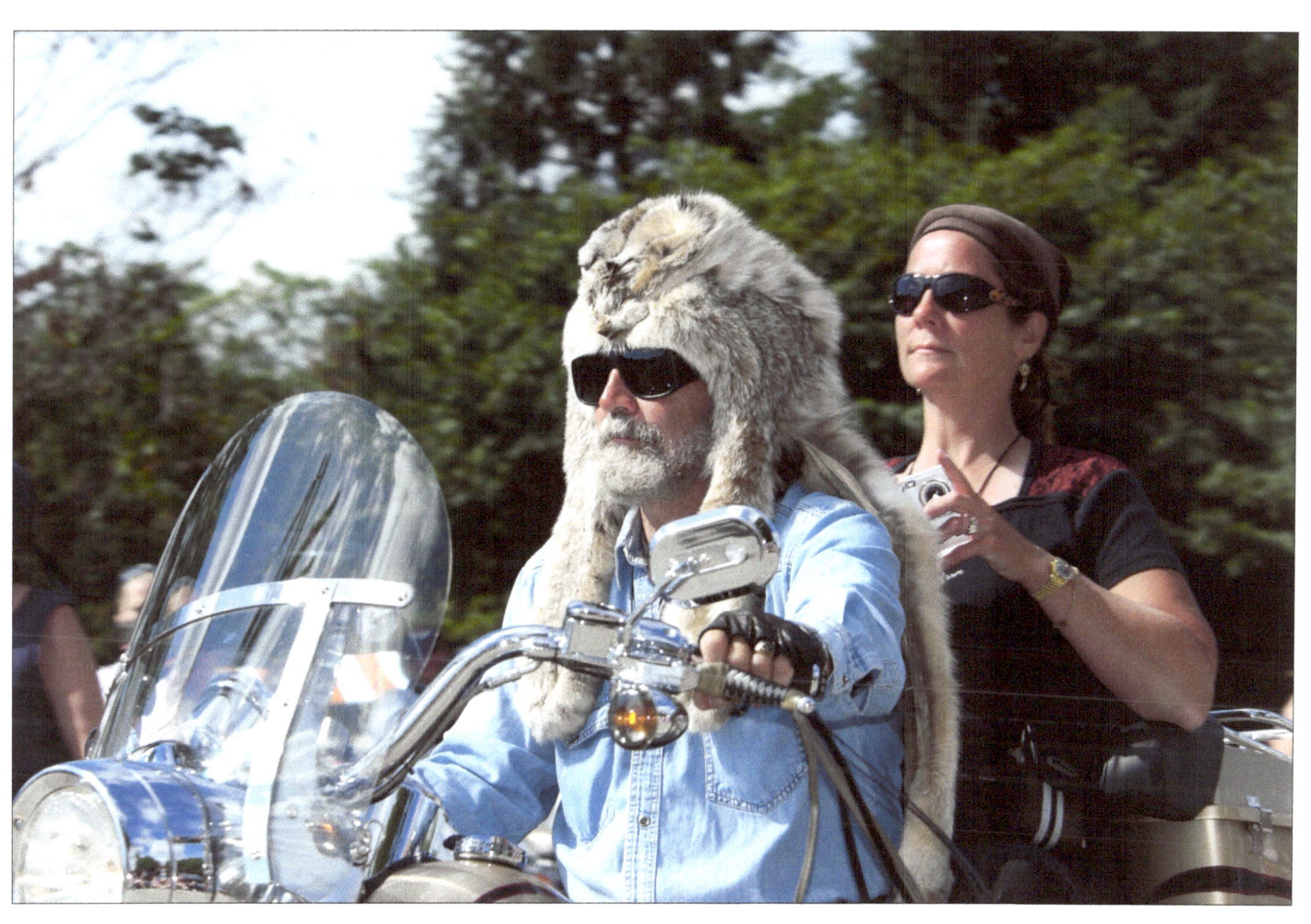

Most motorcycle problems

    are caused by

the nut that connects

    the handlebars to the saddle.

    —Author Unknown

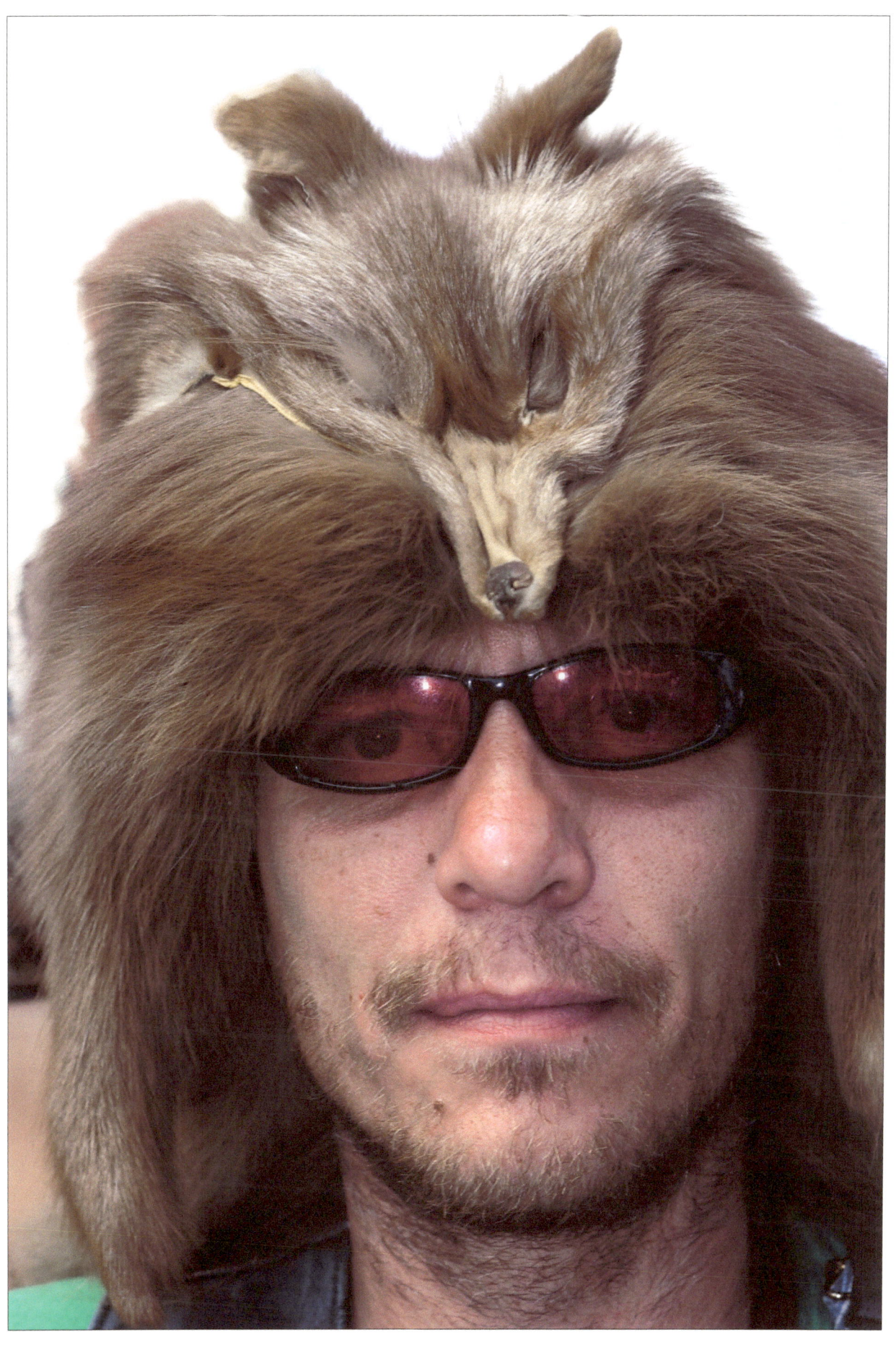

FACES OF HARLEY

If the bike isn't braking properly,

you don't start by

rebuilding the engine.

—Author unknown

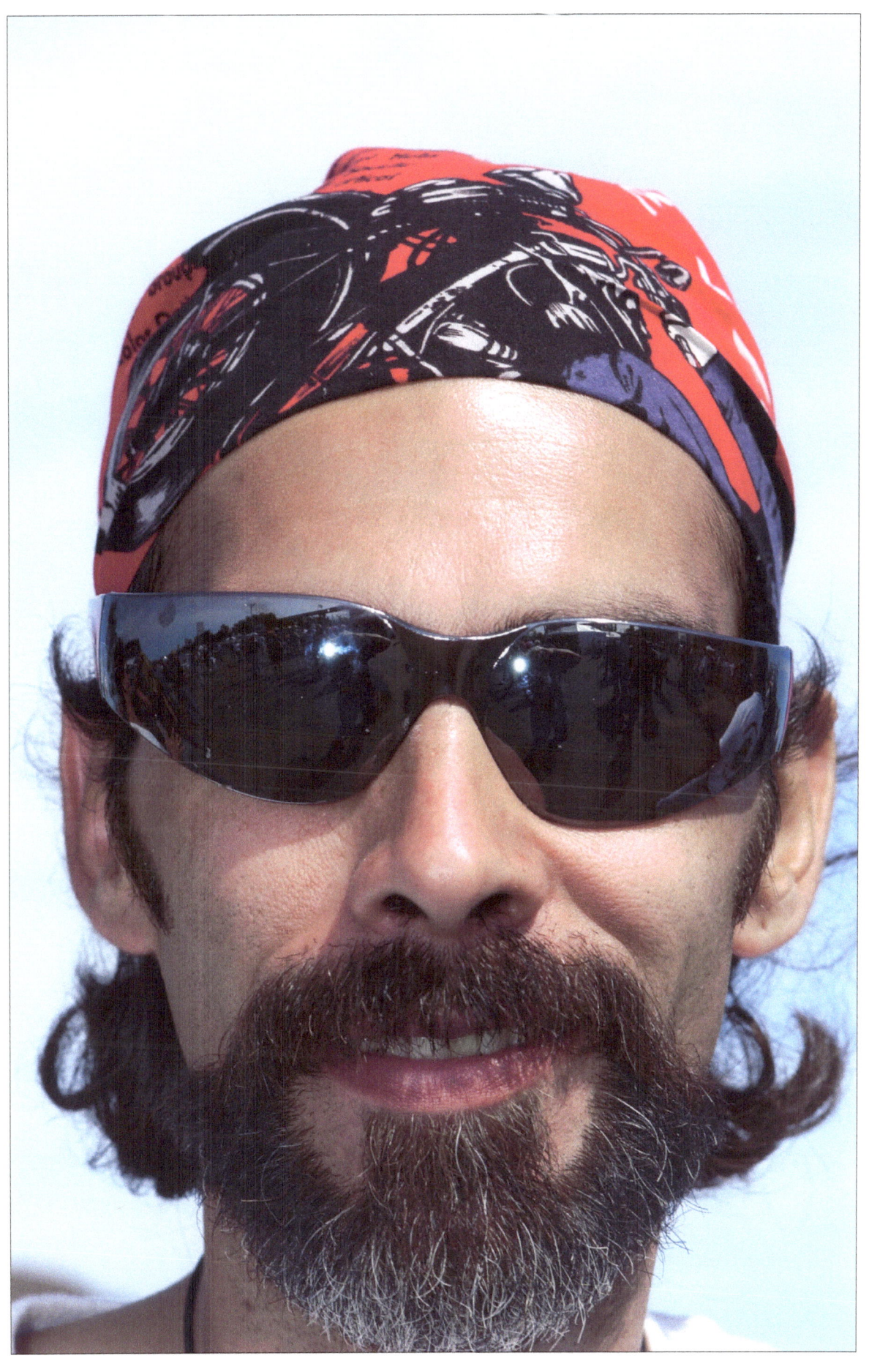

FACES OF HARLEY

Young riders pick a destination and go...

Old riders pick a direction and go.

—Author unknown

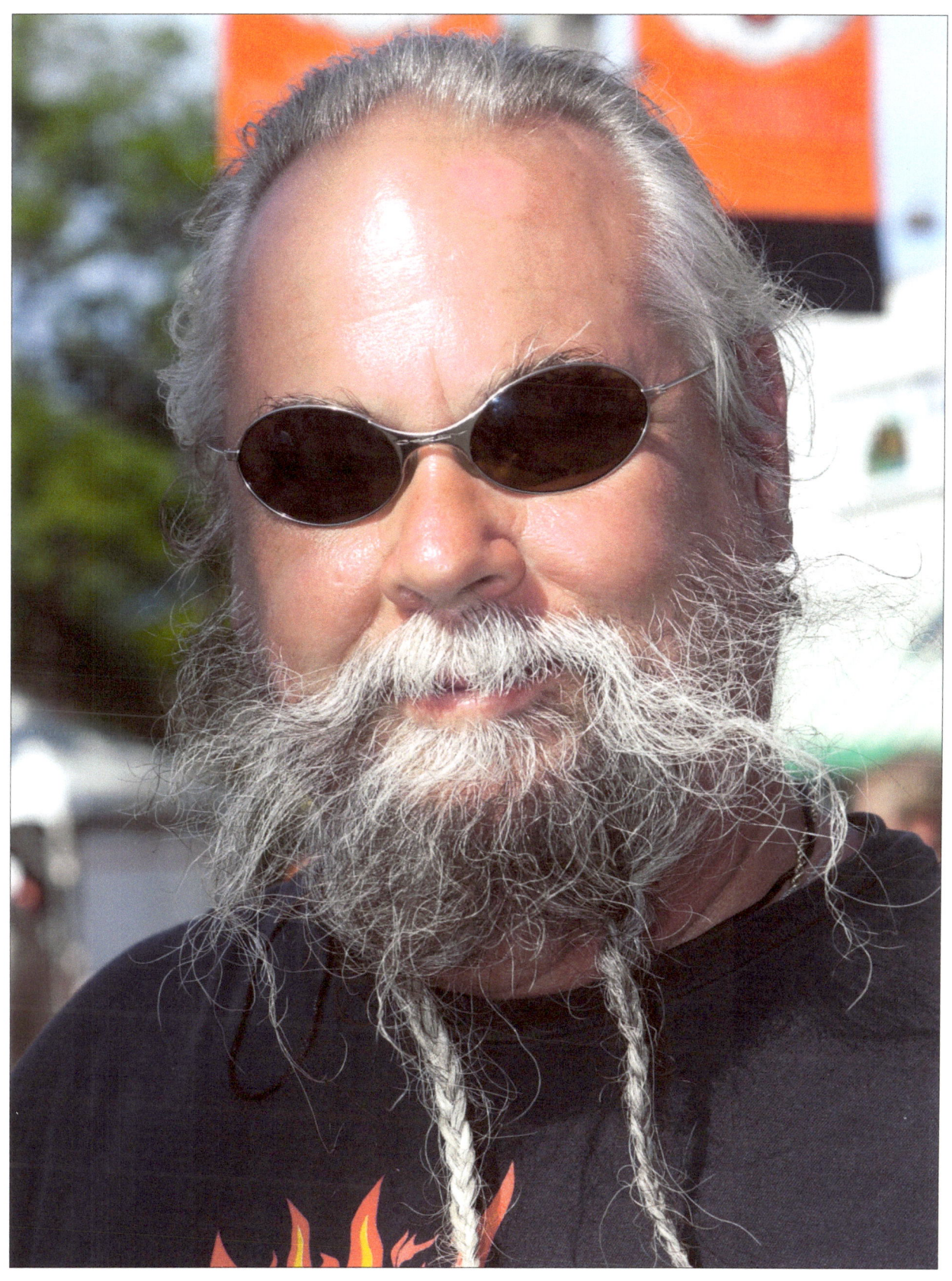

Today's Harley owners share the legacy of the cowboys

of our American West.

They have in common the independent spirit,

cooperative attitude and cowboy-hero mentality

made popular in movies, novels and radio programs.

—Katherine M. Klein

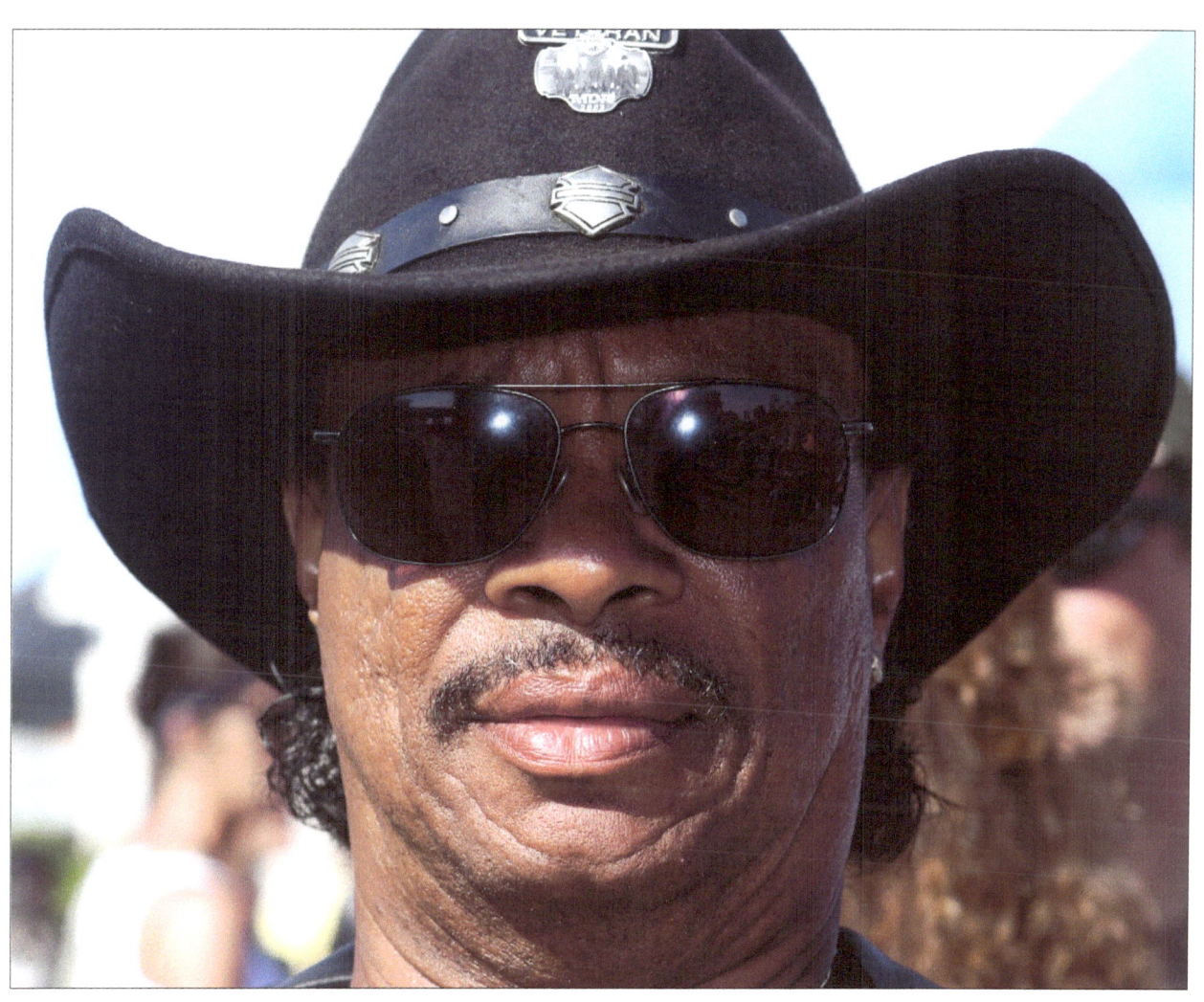

If you ride like there's no tomorrow,

there won't be.

—Author unknown

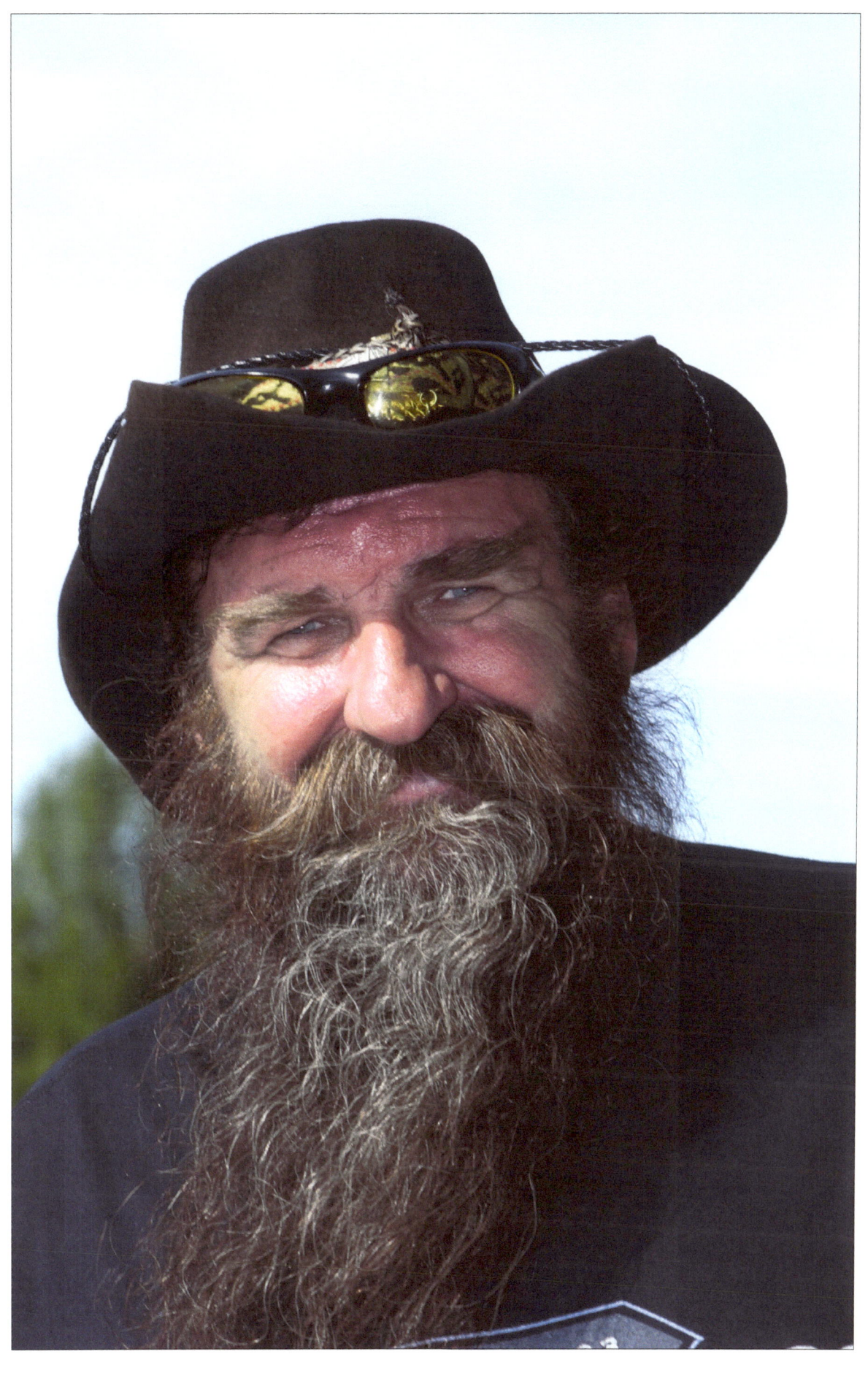

Note to self: Never ride a motorcycle

in stilettos and a miniskirt.

—Maggie Grace

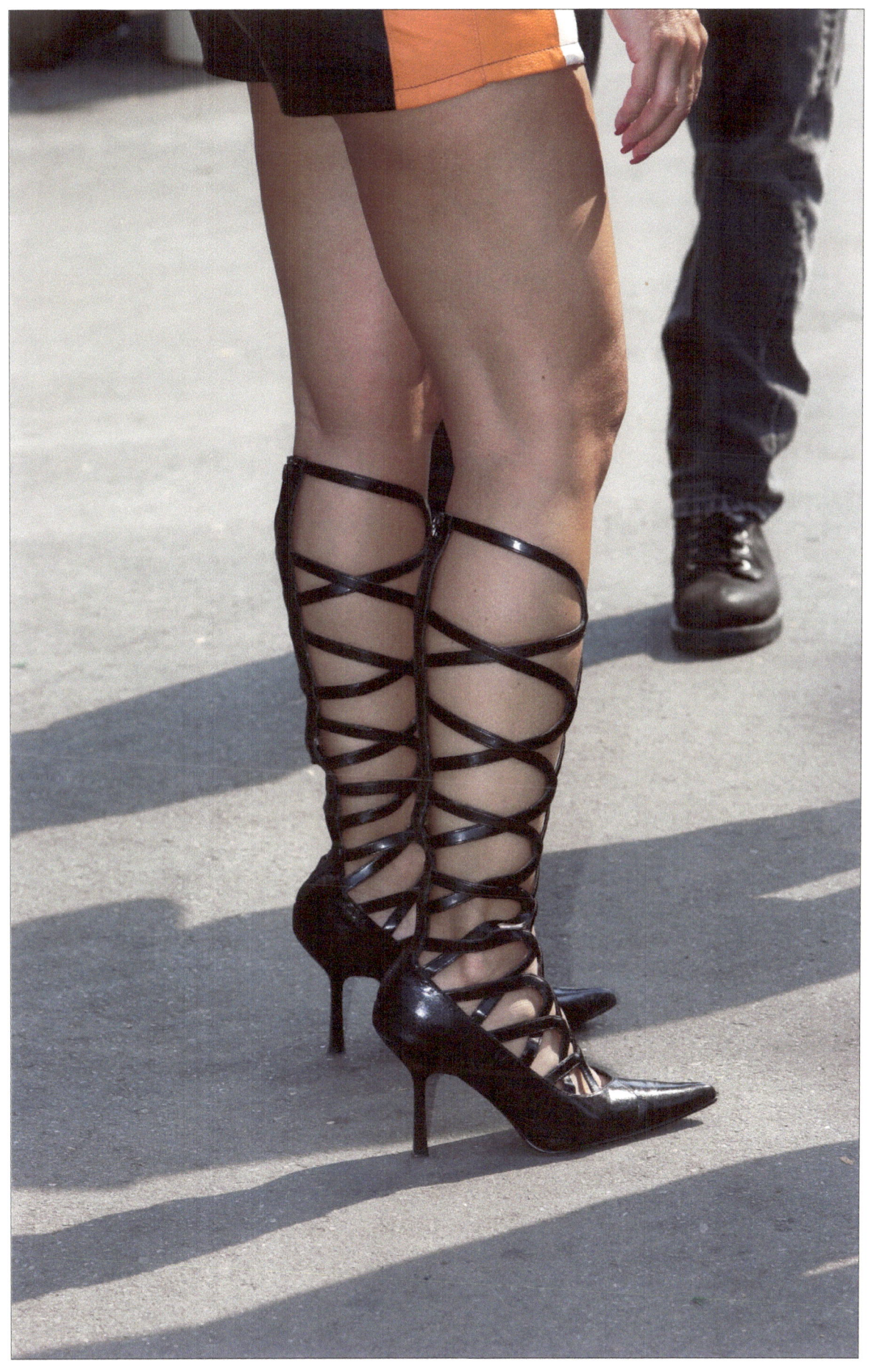

Life should not be a journey to the grave

with the intention of arriving safely

in a pretty, well-preserved body,

rather, to skid in broadside, in a cloud of smoke,

thoroughly used up, totally worn out,

loudly proclaiming,

"WOW, WHAT A RIDE!"

—Hunter S. Thompson

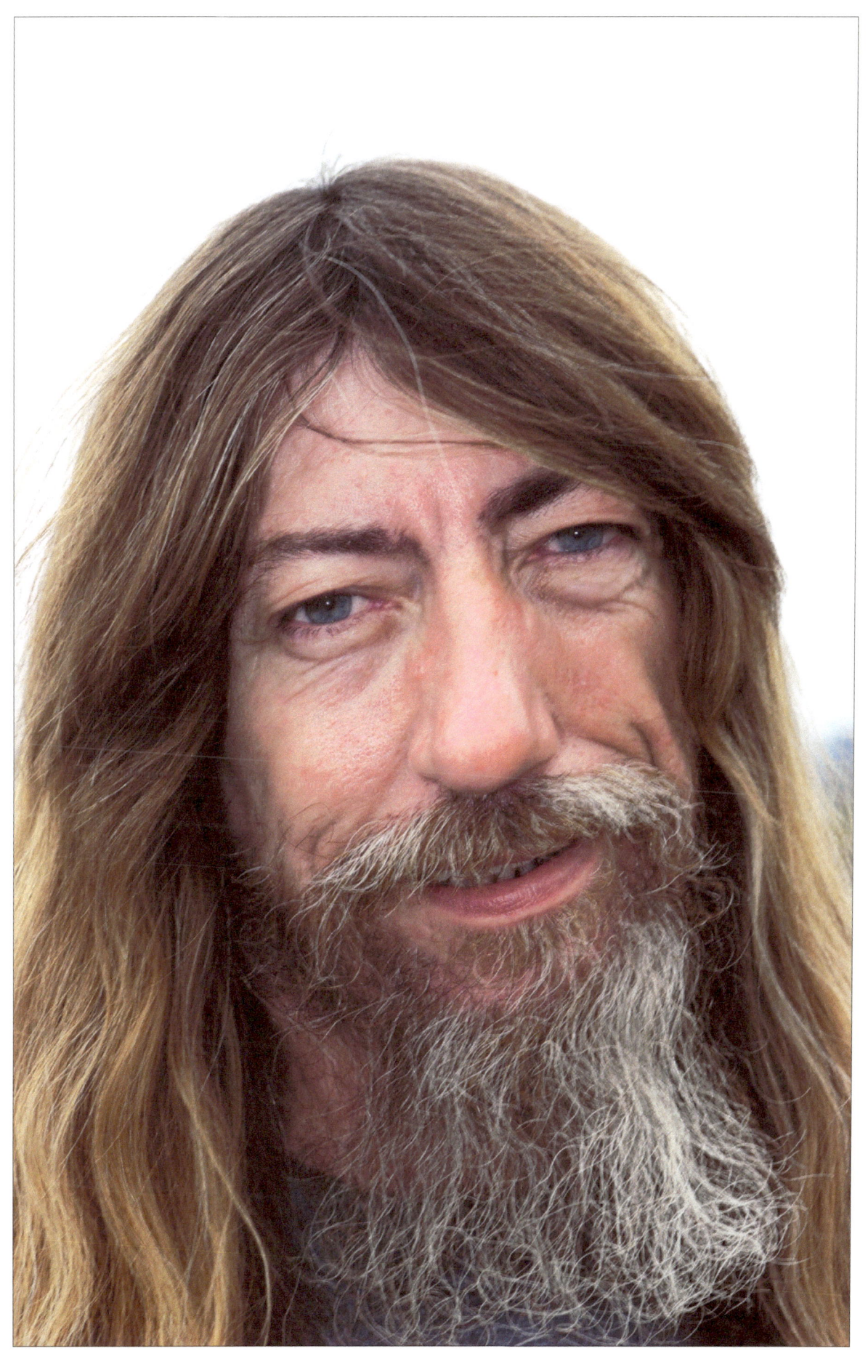

The answer, my friend,

is blowin' in the wind.

—Bob Dylan

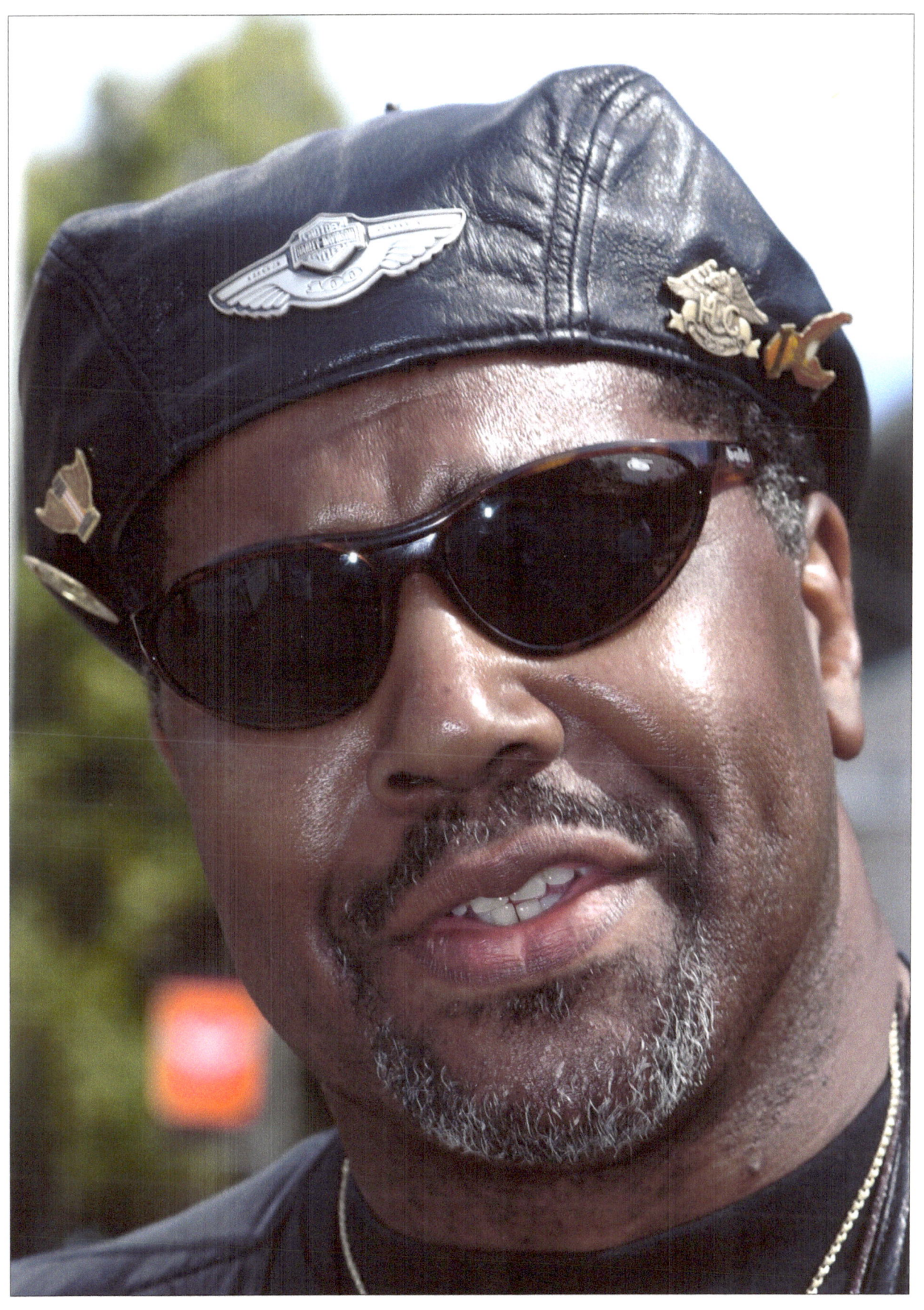

The best way for guys to communicate is

just don't talk to each other for nine hours.

That's why I like long motorcycle rides.

It's a great way for guys to socialize and not socialize.

—Justin Theroux

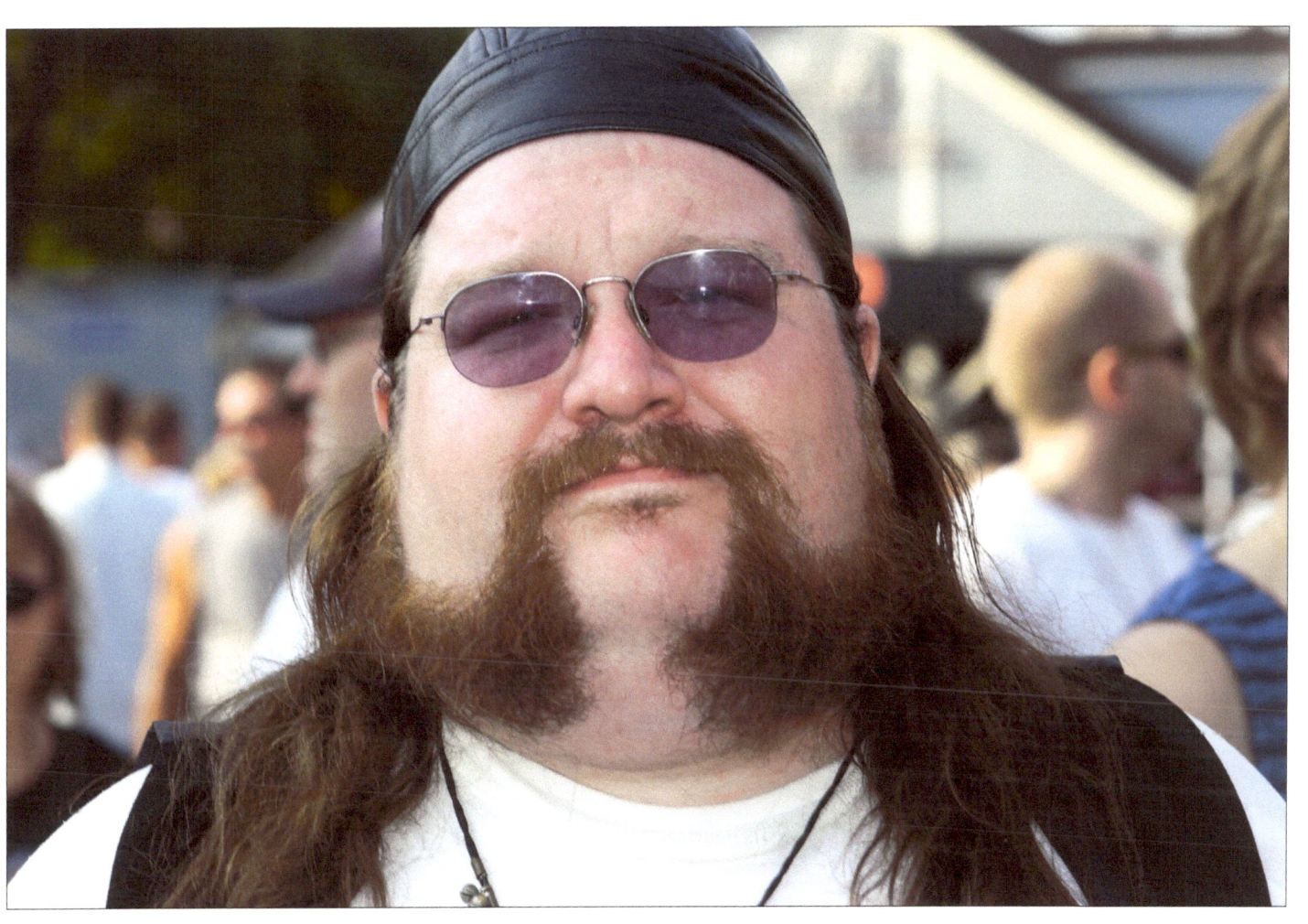

I actually have no aspirations

to ride a motorcycle ever again.

It's exhausting.

You get cold.

—Ally Walker

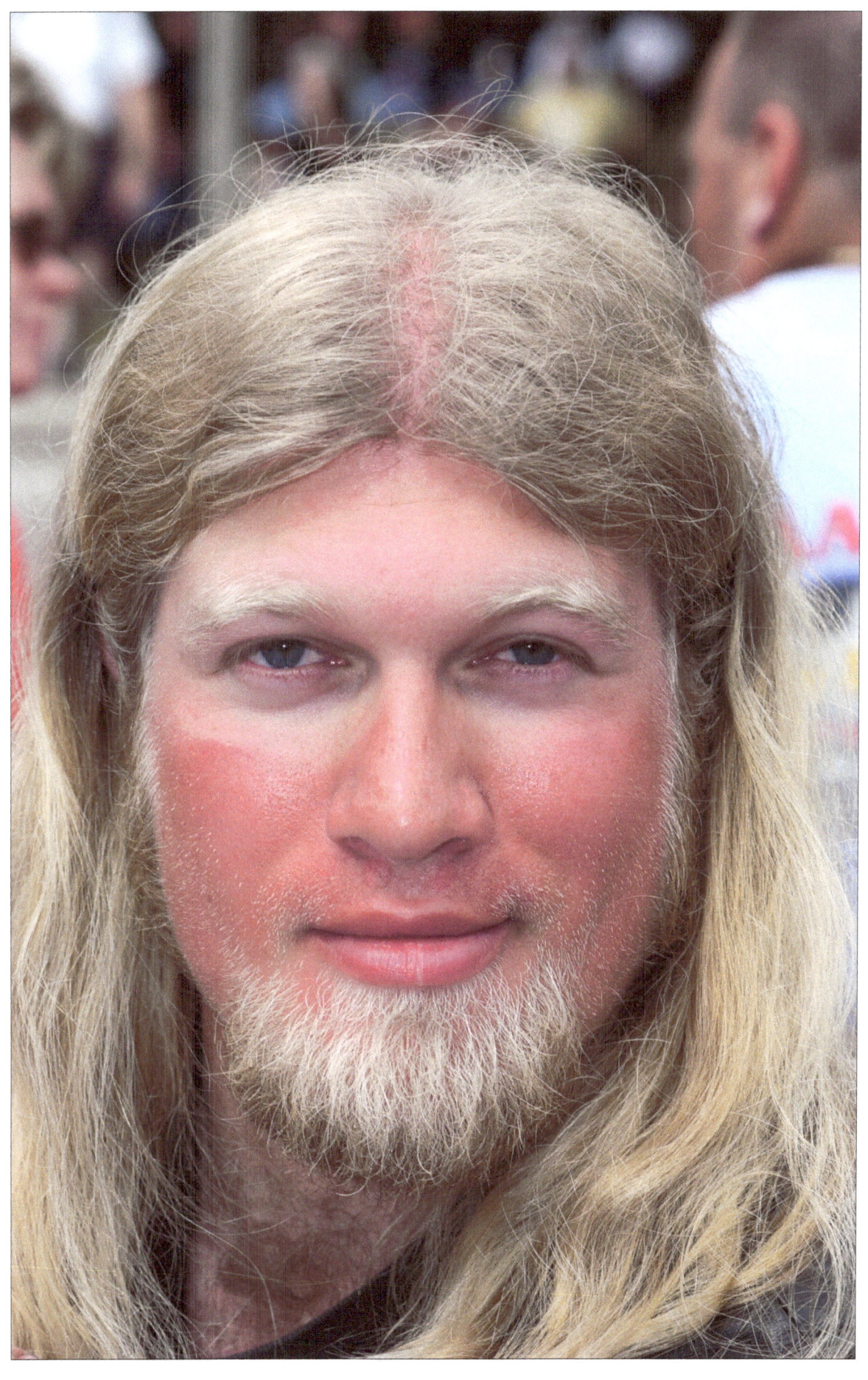

Taking B12 is the price of getting to be vegan,

the way wearing a helmet

is the price of getting to ride a motorcycle,

and giving up alcohol for nine months

is the price of getting to have a baby.

—Victoria Moran

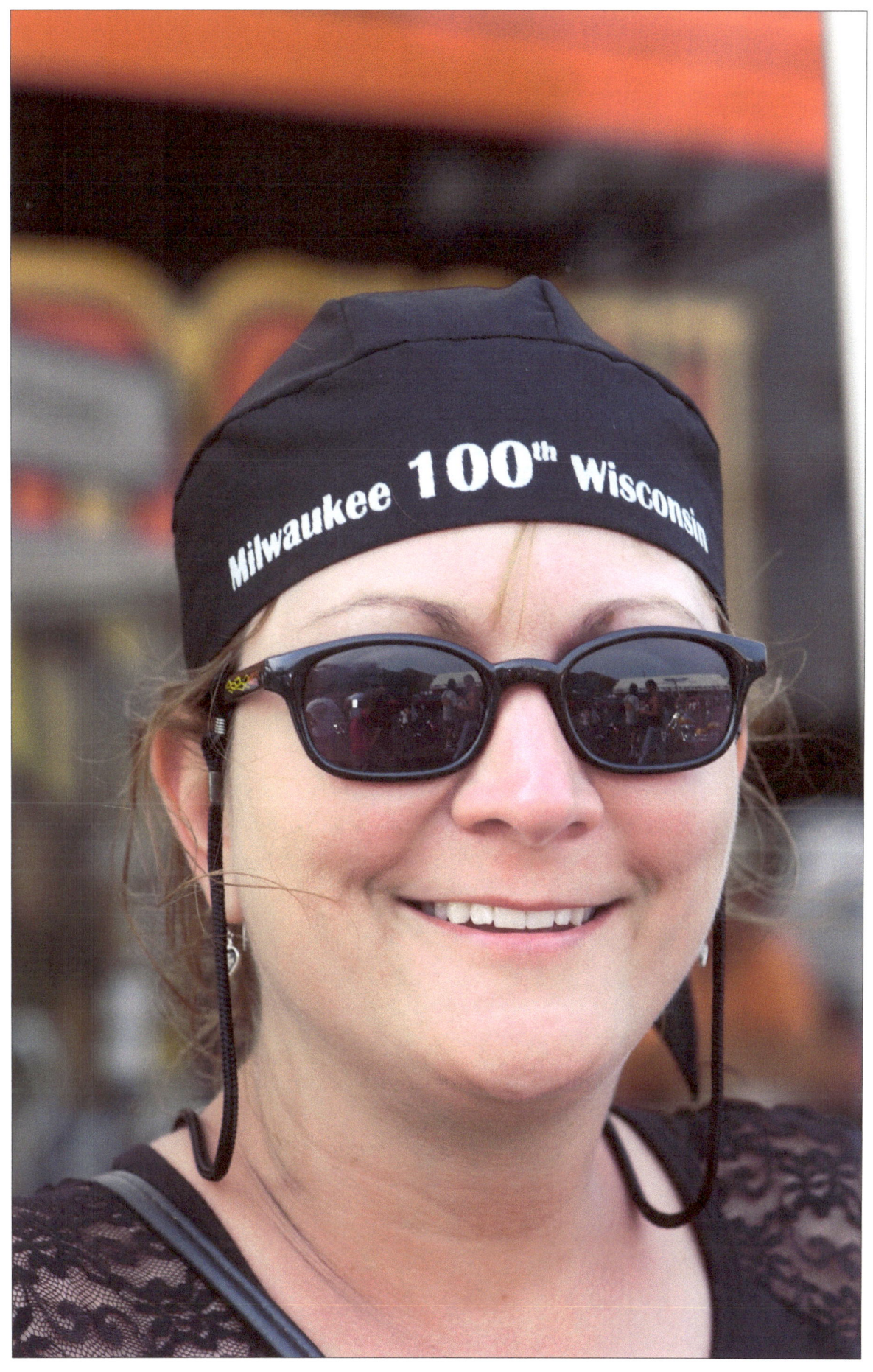

If I weren't doing what I'm doing today...

I'd be traveling around the world

on the back of a motorcycle.

—Donna Karan

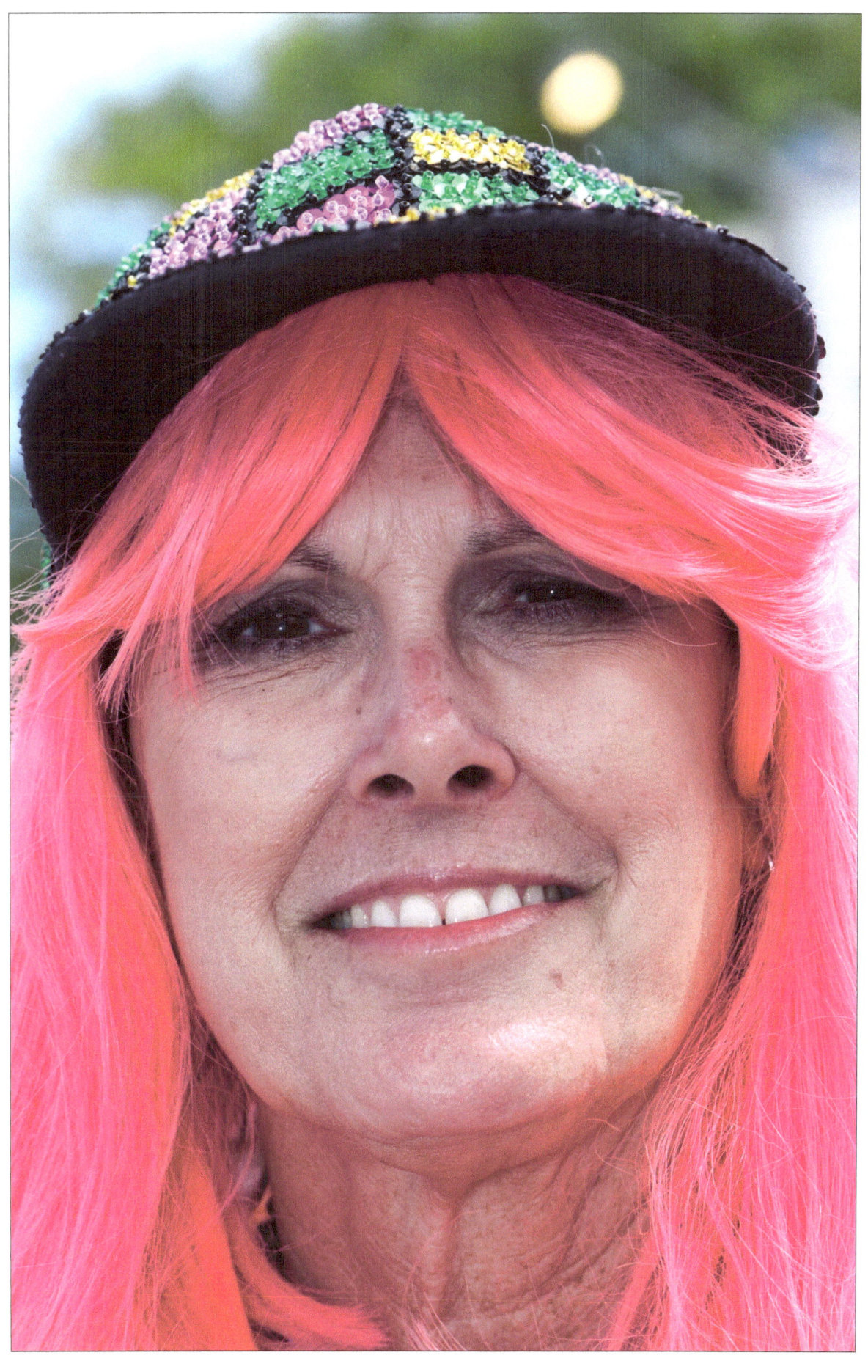

If the person in the next lane

at the stoplight

rolls up the window

and locks the door,

support their view of life

by snarling at them.

—Author unknown

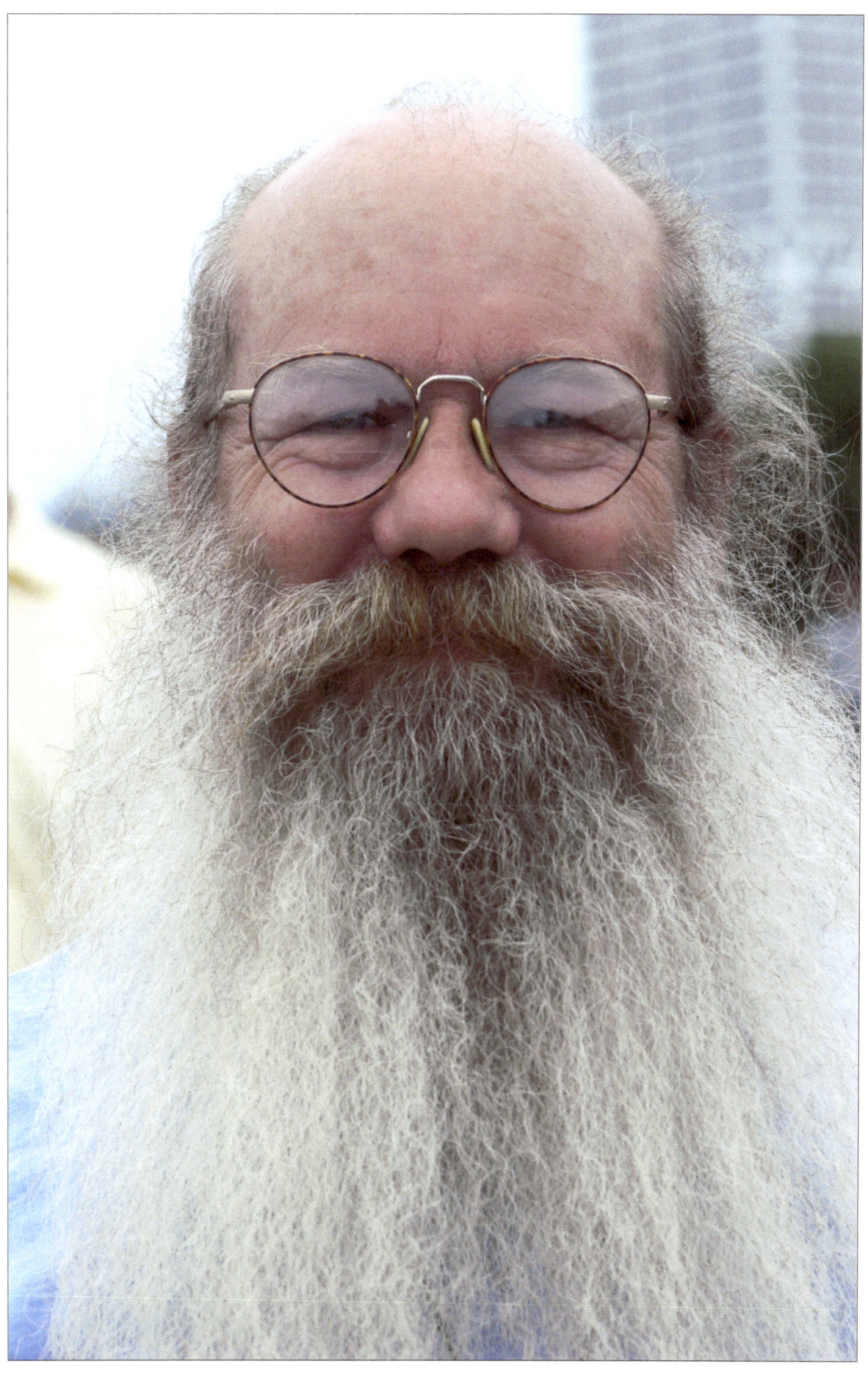

Never trade the thrills of living

for the security of existence.

—Author unknown

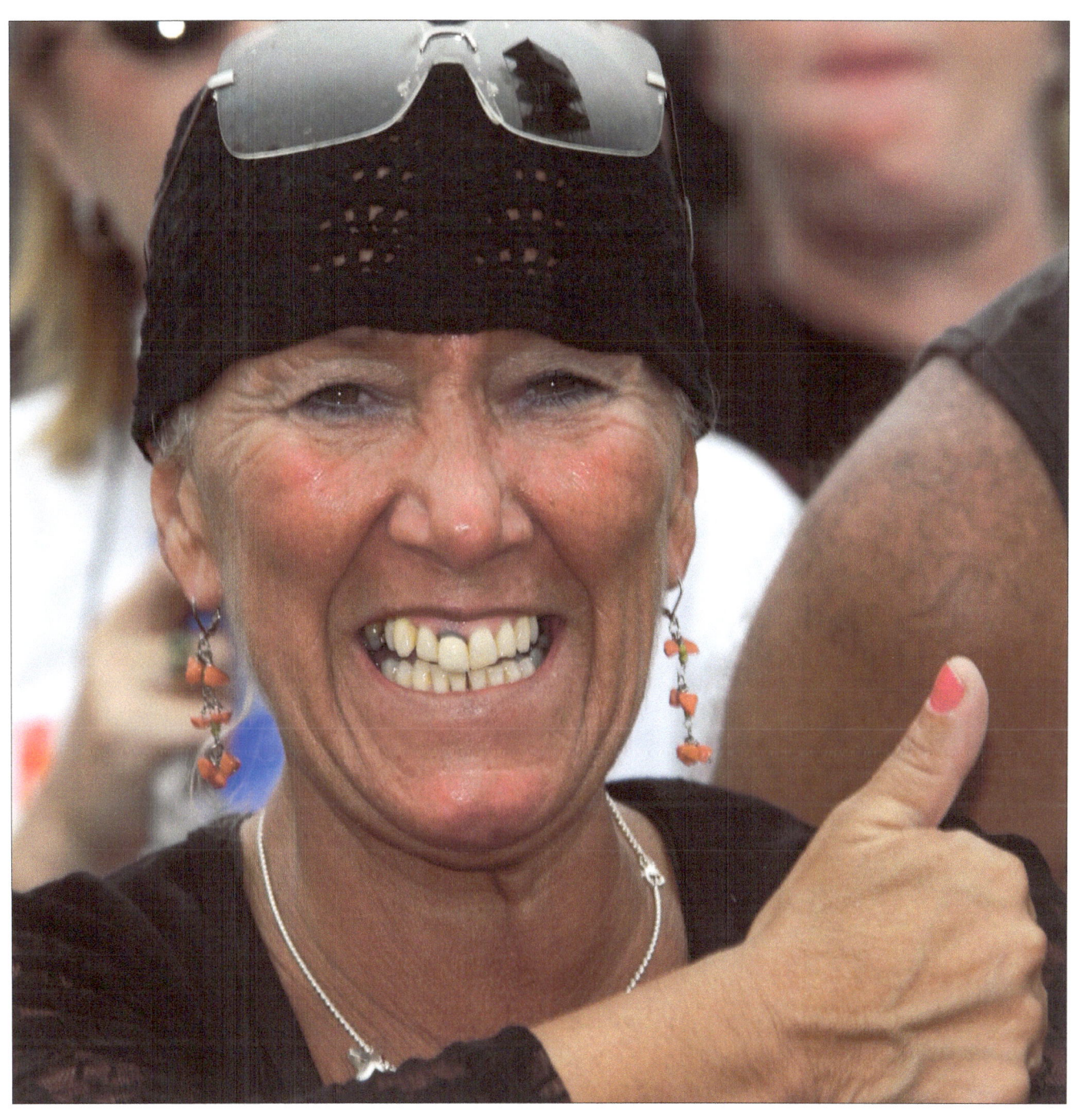

A motorcycle coming down

from 30 feet at 70 mph

gives you a terrible jolt.

—Evel Knievel

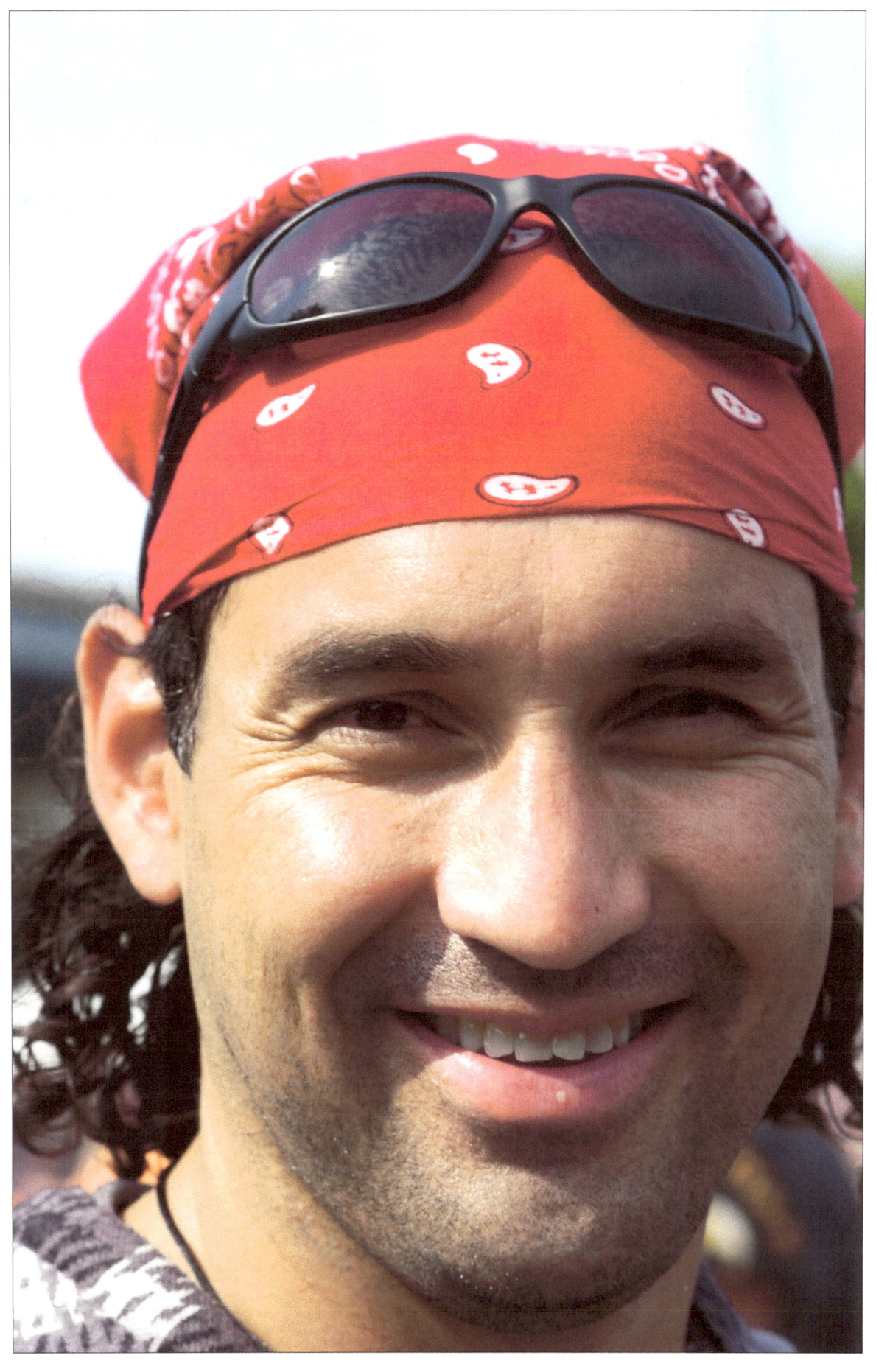

FACES OF HARLEY

The lure of the open road

never goes out of style.

—Author unknown

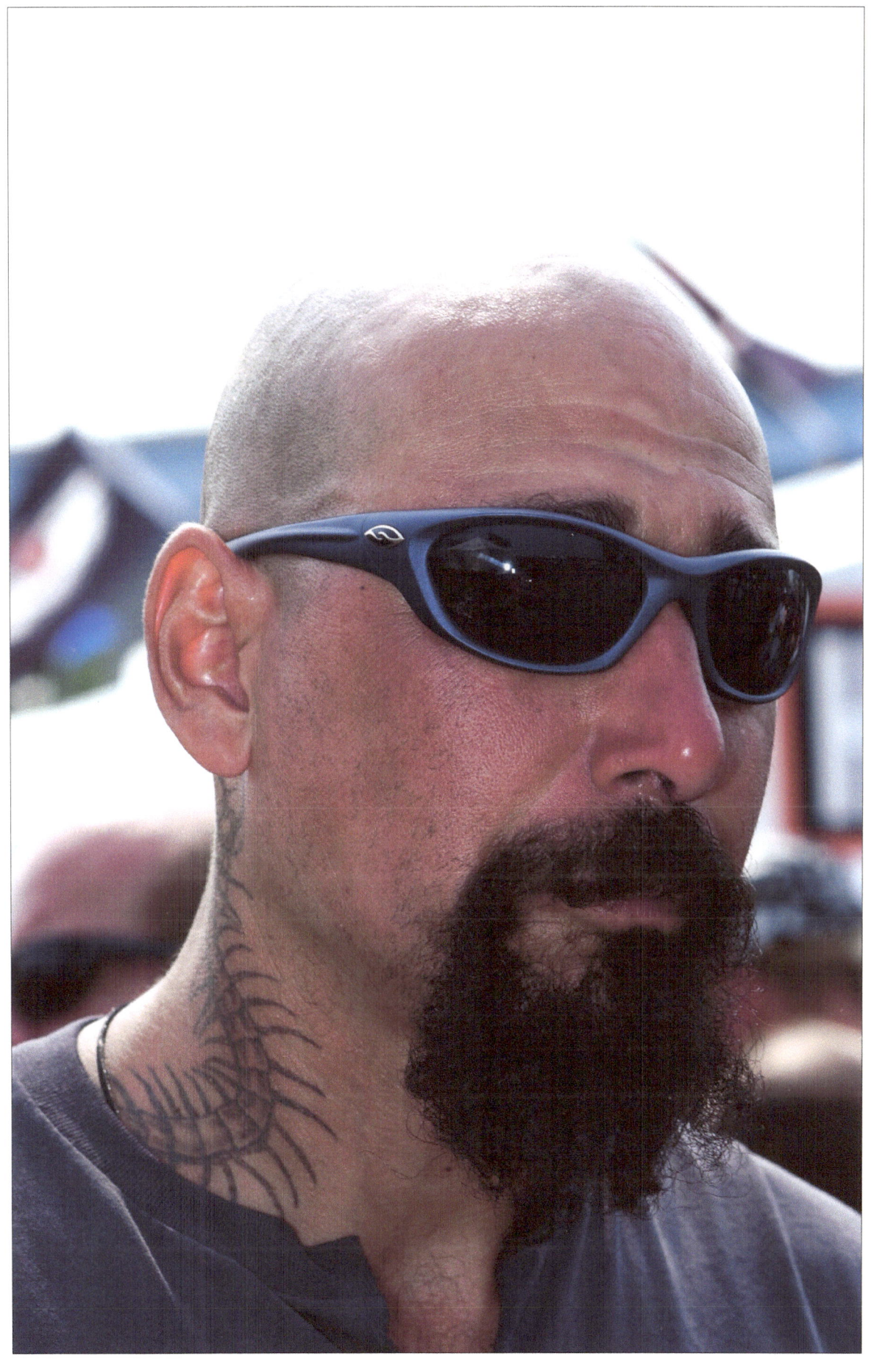

FACES OF HARLEY

Motorcycling is not, of itself, inherently dangerous.

It is, however, extremely unforgiving of inattention,

ignorance, incompetence, or stupidity.

—Anonymous

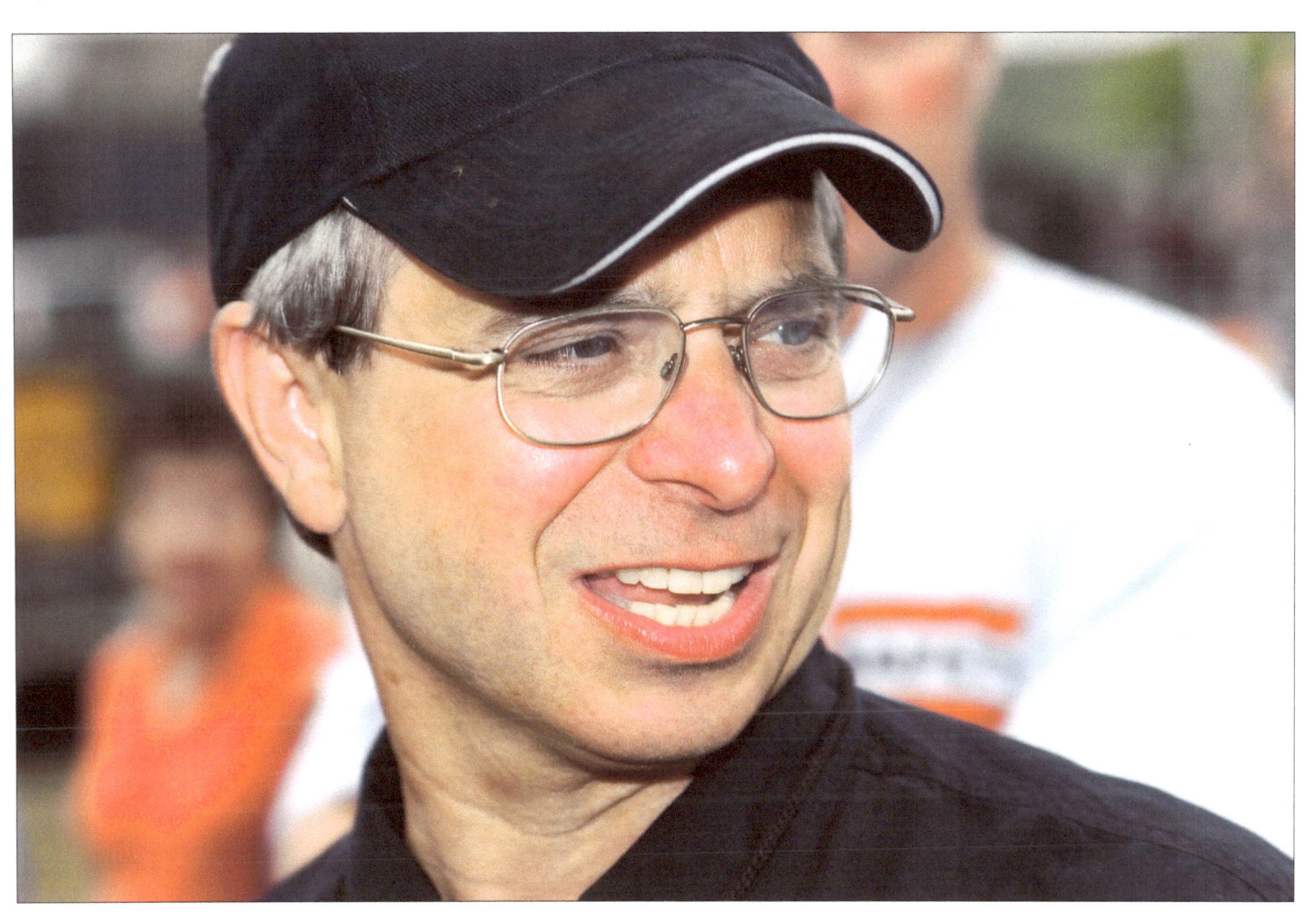

When you're riding lead, don't spit.

—Author Unknown

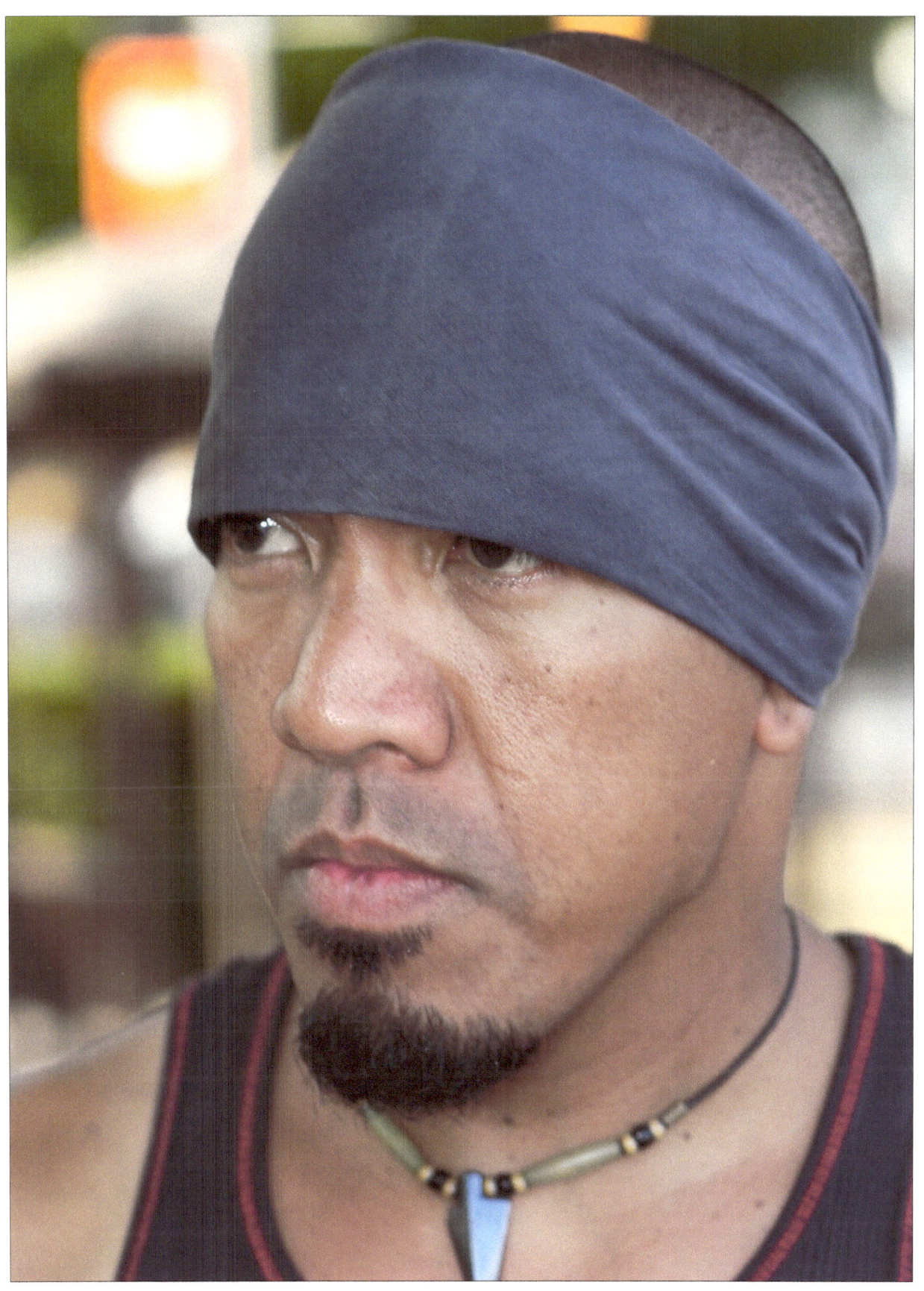

FACES OF HARLEY

Bikes are like wives…

If it ain't yours, don't touch.

—Author unknown

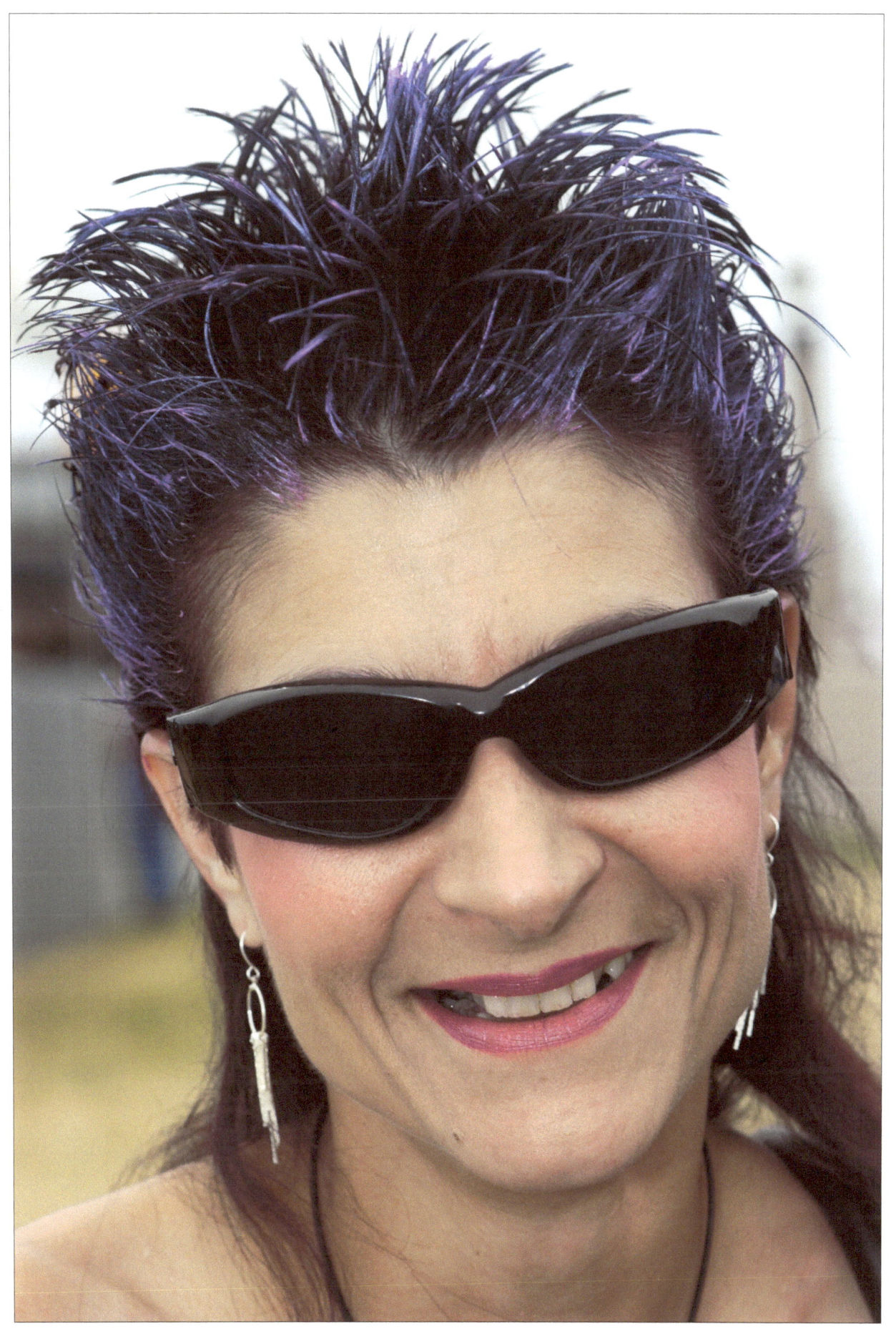

FACES OF HARLEY

I look my best when

I take my helmet off

after a long motorcycle ride.

I have a glow and

a bit of helmet hair.

—Eric Bana

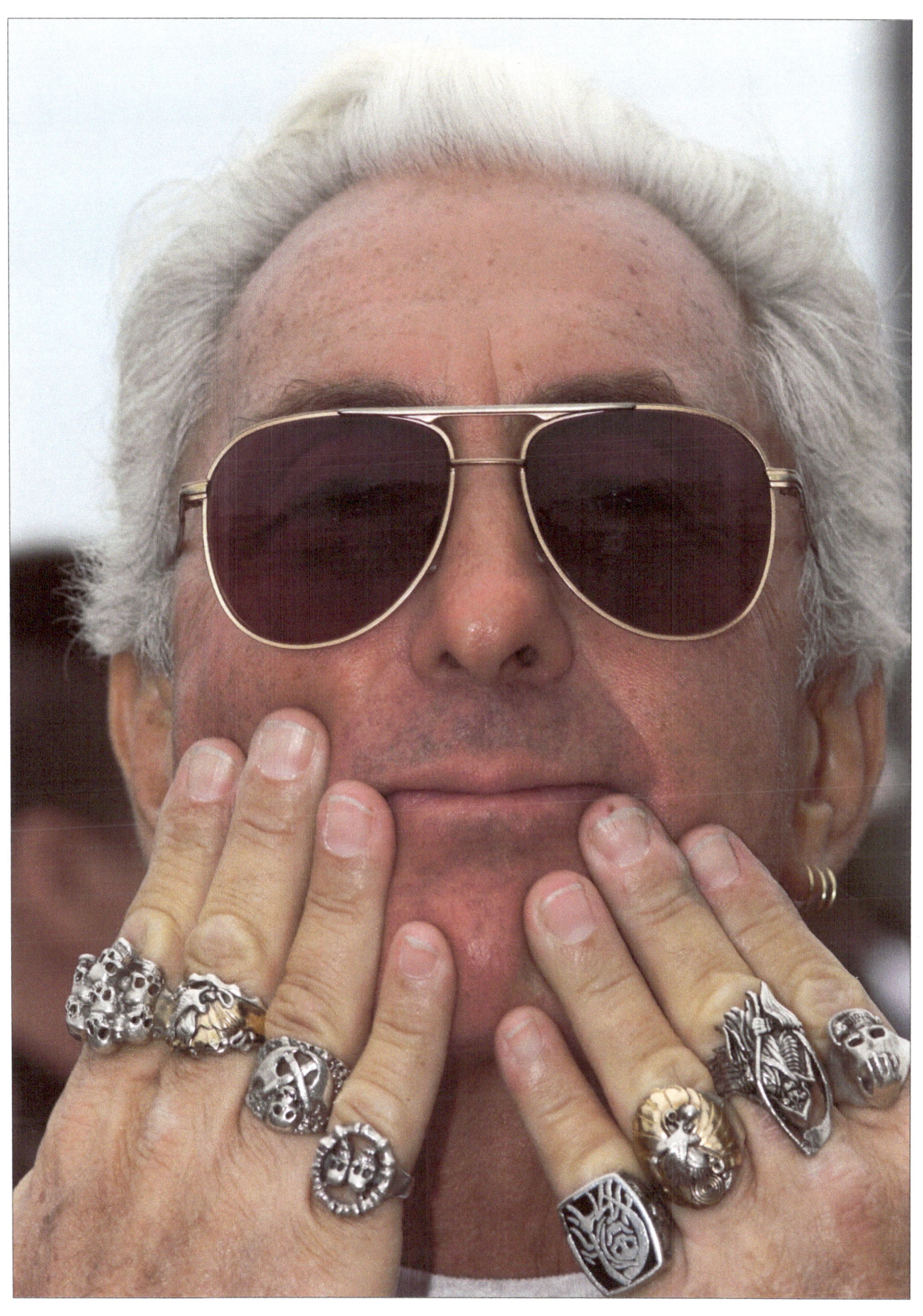

A good rider has balance, judgment,

and good timing.

So does a good lover.

—Author unknown

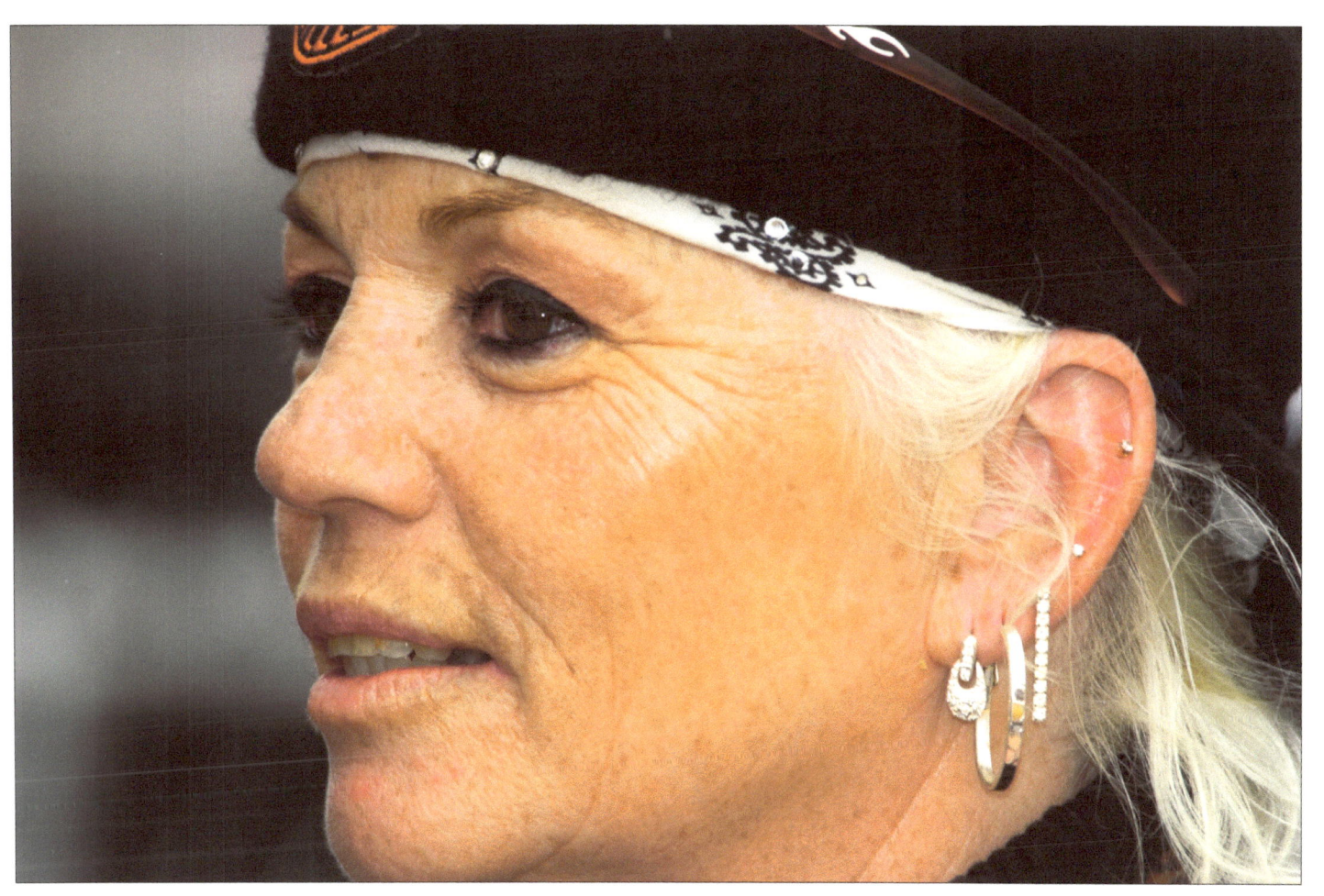

When Valentino Rossi was five,

his dad Graziano built him a go-cart

to discourage him from

getting into bikes.

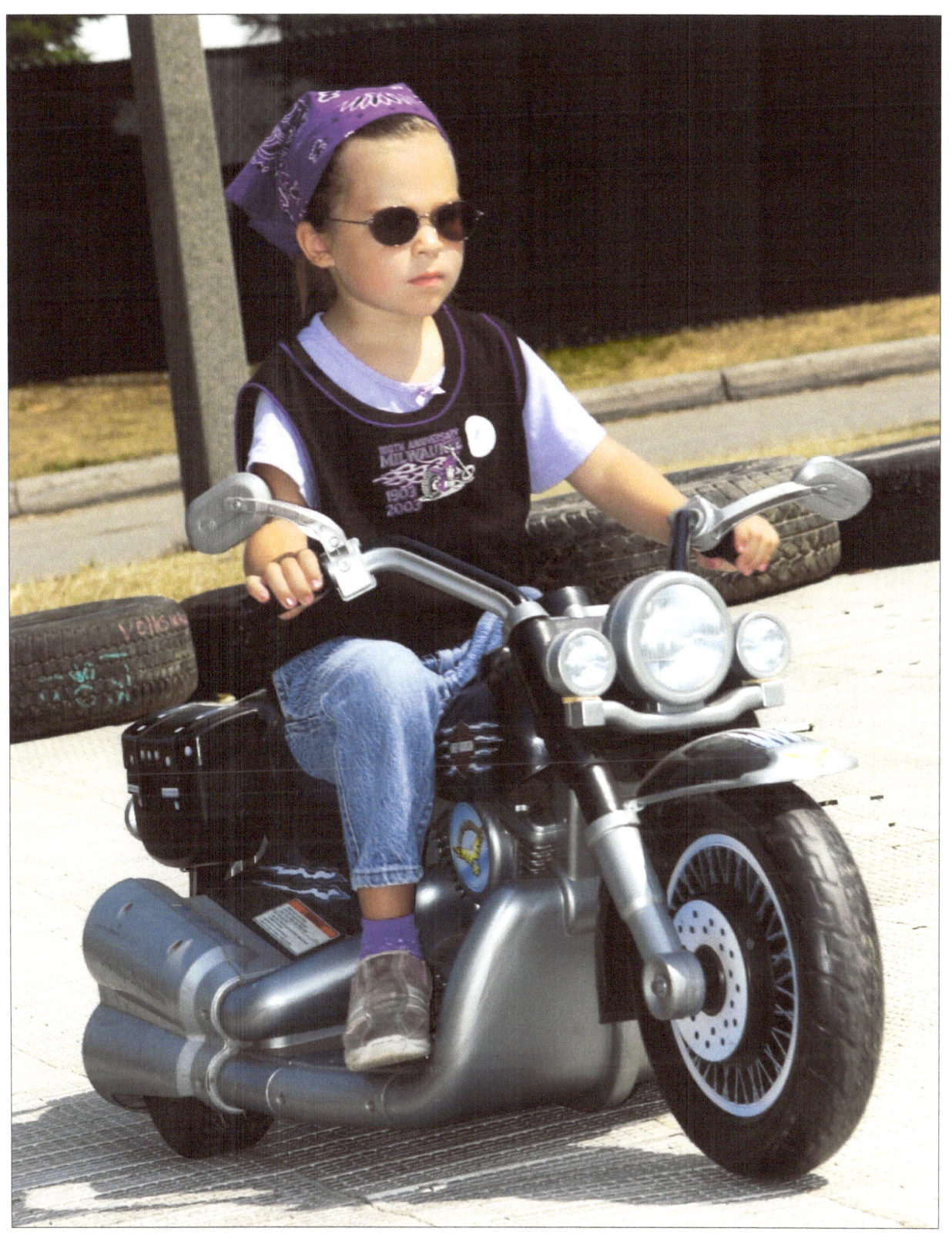

I now know… that my destiny is to travel

—Ernesto Che Guevara

ACKNOWLEDGMENT

My great thanks to Colleen Wilcox for her invaluable suggestions and help in editing.

www.ingramcontent.com/pod-product-compliance
Lightning Source LLC
Chambersburg PA
CBHW051146220526
45473CB00003B/673